MW00637509

the
intentional
spinner

A HOLISTIC APPROACH
TO MAKING YARN

JUDITH MacKENZIE McCUIN

INTERWEAVE.
interweavebooks.com

the intentional spinner

spinner

A HOLISTIC APPROACH TO MAKING YARN

JUDITH MacKENZIE McCUIN

EDITOR Anne Merrow
COVER & INTERIOR DESIGN Pamela Norman
PHOTOGRAPHY Joe Coca (except as otherwise noted)

TECHNICAL PHOTOGRAPHY Ann Swanson
TECHNICAL EDITOR Abby Franquemont
PRODUCTION DESIGN Katherine Jackson

Text © 2009 Judith MacKenzie McCuin
Photography © 2009 Interweave Press LLC
Illustrations © 2009 Interweave Press LLC

All rights reserved.

Interweave Press LLC
201 East Fourth Street
Loveland, CO 80537-5655 USA
interweavebooks.com

Printed in China by Asia Pacific Offset.

Library of Congress
Cataloging-in-Publication Data

McCuin, Judith MacKenzie.
  The intentional spinner : a holistic ap-
proach to making yarn / Judith
MacKenzie McCuin, author.
     p. cm.
  Includes index.
  ISBN 978-1-59668-080-7 (pbk.)
  1. Hand spinning. 2. Spun yarns. I. Title.
TT847.M42 2008
746.1'2--dc22
                    2008014306

10 9 8 7 6 5 4 3 2 1

acknowledgments

THIS BOOK HAD TWO fairy godmothers, Amy Clarke Moore and Liz Gipson, who encouraged me to write this book and helped me through the initial processes. Many thanks for all your support and brainstorming.

And a very sincere thanks to my two intrepid editors: Anne Merrow, whose job it has been to bring form to my words and ideas, and Abby Franquemont, whose technical editing enriched this book greatly. Thanks also to Ann Swanson for her great technical photographs.

I owe a great deal to Dr. Michael L. Ryder for his research and insights on sheep and wool development. To Glen Eidman, developer of the CVM breed, and to Dr. C. Leroy Johnson for so generously sharing their great depth of knowledge on sheep and fiber production, my deepest thanks.

Thanks to my companions on the road, students, mentors, and vendors who make my life so rich and rewarding. I'm a lucky woman. Thanks especially to Kathryn Alexander, Rosemary Brock, Nancy Bush, Maggie Casey, Jan Chamberlain, Laura Fry, Shane and Shiori Hatagawa, Stephanie Pearl-McPhee, Suzanne Pederson, and Morgaine Wilder for many illuminating late-night discussions on textiles, fibers, and life that have helped me clarify my ideas and intentions for this book.

Thanks to the makers of the beautiful tools I use in this book, which give me so much pleasure in my work: the Clemes family (hand cards); Andrew Forsyth (Dutch combs, minicombs, and Russian paddle combs); Gord Lendrum (folding wheel); Nick McCuin (electric drum carder); Schacht Spindle Co. (bobbin winder, Ladybug, and Schacht-Reeves wheels); and Will Taylor (lazy kate).

And thanks indeed to Linda Ligon, founder of Interweave, whose vision has given spinners a wonderful gathering place and a true community.

To Nick, thanks as always for keeping the home fires burning.

contents

TOP TO BOTTOM: FLAX COUNCIL, ANNE MERROW, JOE COCA, JOE COCA, JOE COCA; OPPOSITE PAGE, JOE COCA

introduction

AS A YOUNG WOMAN, I raised my children on a little island off the west coast of Canada. It was an idyllic life. We lived on the edge of the beach in a little cottage covered—and probably held upright—by roses. I could watch otters and orcas from my studio windows while I spun and wove.

Before my children and I came, the people who lived on this land immigrated from England, traveling "round the Horn" in a sailing ship. They braved the roughest water on earth, hoping to find a new life in a new world. They brought with them their linens, china, carriage horses—all the accoutrements of a civilized life in the 1800s. They brought apple-tree cuttings kept alive on the voyage stuck in raw potatoes, lavender and poppy seeds, rhubarb and roses, all a wild tangled garden when I arrived with my cat, a loom, a spinning wheel, and my two small children.

But long before the first European settlers, other people lived here who had also made a perilous journey to find a new home. They traveled across the open grasslands between Russia and Alaska and down the rim of glacier-free land along the seacoast to where my cottage sat. Over thousands of years, they created a midden that eventually formed the foundation for my home. They carved stone vessels and pestles, made magical petroglyphs. Because textiles leave no surviving shards, we can't know the full extent of their textile use, but we do know from their tools and textile artifacts that they spun and wove.

On my little island, across from the stone church on the road to the ferry landing, a rock ledge slopes down toward the sea. Just below the high-tide line is a perfect round pool about 15 feet across, carved in stone by thousands of years of retting nettle. Along with the towering cedar trees that once swept the shoreline, nettle was a main fiber staple of the area. In the rich soil and gentle climate of the Pacific Northwest, nettles are still abundant

PHOTOGRAPHS COURTESY OF THE AUTHOR EXCEPT NETTLE/DAVE WHITE

and often grow several feet taller than my head.

Nettles were collected in early fall and dried over the winter. In the warm late spring and summer, rain filled the depression in the rock and was heated by the sun. Bundles of dried nettle would be laid in the warm rainwater. Sitting across from one another around the pool, women held a long cedar plank that was flat on the top and curved on the bottom. They pounded the nettle stalks to release the strong bast fibers between the outer coating of vegetable material and the pithy inner core.

After washing the loosened materials away in the salty water of the tide, they stretched the nettle fibers to dry on the thorny dog-rose bushes. Day after day, they pounded and rinsed and dried, until only the long, silky nettle fibers were left. Gradually, the natural depression was enlarged and shaped by the motion of the cedar boards. Thousands of years of pounding nettle carved this perfect stone bowl on the edge of the sea.

Nettle was the fabric of their life. Spun into a firm two-ply by thigh-spinning or spindle-spinning, nettle was used to make incredibly durable fishnets, traps, and weirs to harvest the fish that formed the main staple of their diet. Baskets of cedar, cherry bark, and nettle were used for food collection and storage. Because the steadily wet climate along the Pacific Coast made the use of animal skins impractical, these fibers also formed the basis of their clothing. Early people on the West Coast created capes, wraps, and hats from the fibers around them.

I learned about spinning nettle long before I found the stone pool on my island, even before I learned to spin, from one of the wonderful stories my grandmother told. It was a magical tale about a young woman's quest to rescue her seven brothers, who had been turned into swans by their evil stepmother. To rescue them, the young woman had to collect nettle, spin it into yarn, and knit seven shirts out of the nettle yarn—all the while remaining mute.

Many adventures later, her muteness (and perhaps her knitting) caused her to be tied to a stake on the village green to be burned as a witch. But she continued to knit.

Seven swans flew over the village on their spring return to the north and circled her. She threw the shirts up to them, and they turned back into handsome young princes and saved the day. They lived happily ever after, even the youngest prince, who had feathers instead of fingers on his left hand. His sister didn't have quite enough nettle yarn to finish the sleeve of his sweater!

Apart from fairy tales, nettle was an important fiber for early European cultures. Using methods similar to those from the Pacific Northwest, nettle was harvested and spun to make strong, long-wearing yarns. In many European cultures, nettle fiber was considered to be stronger than flax. It was used for many of the fabrics that flax is now used for (clothing, sailcloth, ropes, household linens), but most often for making fishnets; in fact, the word "net" is derived from "nettle." Nor does the story of nettle end in Northern Europe. Years ago, I found an ancient Chinese tapestry that shows dragons coming out of the sea and flying through clouds. Each dragon is ornately woven from a textured nettle thread. China and India have a long history of nettle textiles, and I have recently seen elegant nettle fabrics from Nepal.

The nettle story forms a circle of sorts, the type of circle that has always seemed to me full of mystery and wisdom. The paths of plants, animals, and humans crisscross the planet, intersecting and interconnecting, creating a beautiful and intricate pattern. It reminds me that we are infinitely more similar to one another than we are different.

In the creation myths from many cultures, a spinner is a symbol of creation and change. And here, in the modern world, a love of textiles forms a web that connects us beyond the limitations of gender, race, and belief systems.

The history of fibers and spinning is the history of the world; handspinners have a lineage that stretches back through time, linking us to thousands of years of spinning technology and knowledge. The forces at work in the world and in your fibers are constant and steadfast, shaping your hands and your work as they have always.

～ Judith MacKenzie McCuin

CLOCKWISE FROM TOP LEFT: FLAX COUNCIL OF CANADA AND FLAX CANADA2015 / MARTIN FIRUS / DANIEL MAR /ANN SWANSON

the nature of fibers

PLINY, THE FIRST-CENTURY ROMAN
traveler, naturalist, and textile aficionado, said that
there were four important fibers in the ancient
world, two animal and two vegetable. He referred
to wool and silk, cotton and flax. A few fibers have
been added since Pliny's time—like Angora rabbit,
bison, and manufactured fibers—and others have
been largely lost, including cedar bark, mountain
goat, kudzu, and wisteria. Nevertheless, some two
thousand years later, Pliny is still basically correct;
wool, silk, cotton, and flax are still the basis of most
of the world's textiles.

Fibers can be divided into three main groups:
cellulose-based, protein-based, and manufactured
(fibers made in a laboratory). Chapters 1 and 2
explore the properties of cellulose and protein fibers,
essential for thousands of years. Chapter 3 discusses
manufactured fibers with a longer history than
you might expect. Chapter 4 examines fiber from a
scientific perspective, exploring why fibers behave as
they do.

CHAPTER ONE

cellulose

Cellulose is the primary building block of all green plants, forming the structure of the plants' cell walls. Cellulose has many uses in the modern world. It is the major component of cotton, linen, and ramie textiles, and also of paper and cardboard products. Cellulose is used in making detergents and shampoos because it attracts and surrounds dirt, making it easy to rinse away. When converted to a liquid by treating it with a variety of chemicals, cellulose can be extruded into a clear cellophane or a variety of rayon fibers. In the world of handspinning, cellulose fibers come from three sources: bast fibers, seed-hair fibers, and regenerated fibers from a variety of sources. (For in-depth information about regenerated cellulosics, see Chapter 3.)

GEOF KIME, STEMERGY.COM

These bast fibers (from a hemp plant) are loosening from the pithy core.

Bast: The First Fibers

NETTLE, FLAX, HEMP, AND RAMIE

Bast fibers are the skeletal parts of plants that hold the plant upright and in some cases give structure to the leaves. These fibers are found sandwiched between the outer bark or vegetable covering on stems and leaves and the plant's pithy core. Think of a stalk of celery: when you break a stalk, the stringy bits are the bast fibers. Each individual fiber is actually a bundle of finer fibers glued together with pectin and coated with a varnishlike substance. When the varnish is removed and the pectin dissolved, finer bundles are released. Like Russian dolls, each opening up to reveal a smaller one, bast fibers can contain hundreds of fine bundles, each containing hundreds of even finer fibers.

Flax, hemp, and ramie are well-known prehistoric bast fibers that the textile industry, handspinners, and weavers still use extensively. Because it is difficult to cultivate, nettle isn't used industrially, although indigenous spinners and weavers still use it in Nepal, Tibet, and India.

PROCESSING BAST FIBERS

Bast plants are collected just before the seeds have totally ripened. At this time, the cellulose fibers will have developed enough strength to prevent the stem from breaking easily when bent. (If the seeds are allowed to ripen, the oil will be drawn out of the fiber, and the stem will start to weaken.) The entire plant is pulled out of the soil by hand, taking care to keep the root intact. The plants are hung by the root to dry. Doing so lets the seeds finish ripening and the oils of the plant, which are largely in the root, disperse throughout the stem, keeping the fibers pliable and strong.

Next, the seeds are removed by *rippling*. With the stalks held by the root end, the blossom ends are combed through a hackle or a set of coarse combs. The seeds are saved, both to plant for next year's crop and to eat. (Both hemp and flax seeds are high in healthy oils.)

After the stalks are rippled, they are bundled together and either placed under water or spread out on a fence or in a field,

ANNA YU

flax flower

flax straw

strik

cellulose

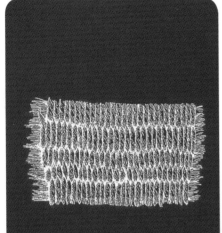

prehistoric bast

BAST FIBERS were the first fibers that humans used. During the time of the woolly mammoth and the cave bear, before the use of metals, people spun and wove bast fibers and had well-developed cording (rope-making) and plaiting (braiding) techniques as well. The use of bast fibers virtually covered the globe; bast fiber samples have been found in fragments from the earliest ruins in Egypt, Mexico, the southwestern United States (Arizona), Peru, Switzerland, China, Russia, and Scandinavia.

Though no one can know for certain when or where the first curious mind discovered that twisting these fibers produced a useful thread, each spinner shares in that exciting moment of discovery as she learns to spin. Sisal, jute, milkweed, sunflower, yucca, agave, New Zealand flax, pineapple, artichoke, coconut—the list of bast fibers that we have used is endless, a tribute to the resourcefulness and inventiveness of spinners everywhere.

nineteenth-century flax hackle

so that rain and dew can work with bacteria and mold to dissolve the outer vegetable coating. This rotting process, called *retting*, causes no damage to the bast fibers, which are impervious to mildew, molds, fungi, and bacteria. Different methods of retting cause color changes in the fiber. Dew retting, which lets weather and oxygen help the bacteria break down the vegetable coating, produces a silvery gray color. Water retting uses warm stagnant water to dissolve the outside layer. Good water-retted fiber is the color of straw. The quality of the water is important. If the water is muddy, the fiber will be a dull gray. If the water contains iron, it can stain and weaken the fiber and also cause *foxing*, the rusting away of the fabric after it's produced. After retting, the dissolved vegetable material is rinsed away and the fibers are dried again.

Next, the stalks are broken to release the bast fibers from the plant's woody core by *scutching*. Scutching can be done by hand, by cracking the stalks over the knee every few inches, or more quickly with a specially designed tool called a *flax brake*. The strong bast fibers are then separated from the pith and any bits of vegetable matter that might remain by *hackling*. The fibers are combed through finer and finer hackles, blossom end first, then the root. Combing releases the strong spinnable fibers from the broken pith and begins the separation of the individual fiber bundles into increasingly finer bundles. Generally it takes six to ten passes between the sets of combs to produce a good spinning fiber.

On each pass, the waste is set aside; most of it can be used. Waste from the first pass is throwaway, historically used along with the *boon* (the woody core of the plant) to fire up the scouring kettle. The second pass

hackling

Comb the fibers through finer and finer hackles, blossom end first, 1 then the root. 2 Combing releases the strong spinnable fibers from the broken pith and begins the separation of the individual fiber bundles into increasingly finer fibers.

rippled flax

can be retted again to make paper. By the third pass, the fibers are smooth enough to make good ropes; by the fourth, rough cloth and rug warps; by the fifth and sixth, clothing. These long fibers, as long as 4 feet (1.2 meters) depending on the type of fiber, are called *line* and are sold in *striks*. Striks maintain the order of blossom to root and are spun from the blossom end. The short fibers from the last two passes are also spinnable; called *tow*, they are used to make a softer, more textured yarn.

NETTLE

The nettle family grows literally worldwide; its thirty to fifty species are native to Asia, Europe, North Africa, and North America. Although its textile use now is mainly historic, at one time it was the most commonly used fiber plant in the world. It's easy to process and spin into exceptionally strong, long-wearing threads. The fiber is impervious to ultraviolet light, mold, mildew, and bacteria. Other than iron contamination, only fire will destroy it.

The decline in the use of nettle is probably linked to its very wildness; it was replaced by flax as we transitioned from a hunter-gatherer to a more agrarian culture. (Although we also collected and used flax before cultivation, flax made the transition from wildness to cultivation more easily than nettle.) Nettle seeds ripen unevenly and spread sporadically, making it a less reliable crop. And no matter how carefully I harvest nettle, I never escape the sting from the spikes of acid on the underside of the leaves. Although the acid becomes inactive as the plant is harvested, it can certainly raise some tender welts before it is gone.

Nettle is still used in many parts of the world that depend on wild gathering as

DAVE WHITE

nettle

cellulose

This dragon, from an ancient Chinese tapestry, is woven from nettle thread.

flax

part of their agriculture for both food and medicine as well as textiles. Nettle yarns for knitting and weaving have become part of the fair-trade movement.

FLAX

Flax has been cultivated for its fiber and seed since Neolithic times. Flax is found in predynastic Egyptian cloth and was used by the Swiss Lake Dwellers. Textile fragments found at Chatalyuk in Turkey—the oldest continually inhabited place on earth—are thought to be flax.

The plant is an annual, sown in the spring and pulled in the fall; it easily reseeds itself, and its seeds can be collected and saved for planting. It has a much wider growing range than nettle and is much more tolerant about the type of soil it will grow in. The stalks grow 2 to 5 feet (.6 to 1.5 meters) tall and have beautiful blue, white, or violet flowers, depending on the variety. The flowers are heliotropic: like sunflowers, they follow the sun's direction and close up at night.

The many varieties of flax have different qualities and yield different products. Some are primarily grown for seed, which in turn produces linseed oil, paper, paint, birdseed, food additives, dietary supplements, linoleum, and even high-tech medicines. These plants grow multiple stalks from a single root and are somewhat bushy in appearance. Flax can be grown in huge fields and harvested by machine or by hand to make a strong, serviceable yarn.

For fine cloth, however, finer fiber is needed. To meet demand for finer and finer fabrics, new cultivars have been developed that grow a single taller and much finer stem. These cultivars produce a fiber called *line flax*, which is longer than 10 inches (25.5 centimeters). Shorter fibers, called *tow*, usually come from the hacklings that produce line flax. The latest development in flax processing, twice-retted flax, is the exception, producing a much finer and shorter high-quality fiber—4 to 5 inches (10 to 12.5 centimeters).

hemp

HEMP

"Hemp" is the name for bast fibers from a large number of plants belonging to the *Cannabis* family. Hemp produces a vast amount of fiber per crop, considerably more than flax and more than four times what a tree can produce on the same land in a year. The fiber can grow to a length of 8 feet (2.4 meters). It is a coarser fiber than flax but stronger and, like all bast fibers, extremely long-wearing. It is easy to release from the plant core. Hemp makes the strongest paper, without the toxic dioxins needed to release cellulose from tree fiber.

Hemp appears to have first been domesticated east of the Caspian Sea and its use spread in all directions. Predynastic grave cloths have been found in Egypt and records of hemp workers, the Kannabarioi, in Ephesus. Records show that hemp was used as early as 2700 B.C. in China. It came to prehistoric Europe from Russia and was used extensively for sails and ropes, giving Scandinavian sea raiders a definite advantage. Columbus, too, much later, sailed with hemp sails and ropes on his voyages to the New World. Thomas Jefferson wrote the U.S. Constitution on hemp paper.

Hemp is grown commercially around the globe, but China is the largest producer—40 percent of commercial hemp fibers come from China. Since World War II, the United States has prohibited growing fiber hemp as a crop for fear of it being used to disguise marijuana, a close cannabis relative. Fiber hemp, however, contains virtually no

flax (twice-retted)

cellulose

tetrahydrocannabinol (THC), the active drug ingredient found in marijuana.

Hemp is grown and processed the same way as flax, and like flax, it has many uses. It has great potential as a bio-fuel; it's also a wonderful candidate for making eco-friendly regenerated cellulose fibers (see Chapter 3).

RAMIE

Ramie is a member of the nettle family. A stingless nettle, it is a beautiful shrub with dark-green heart-shaped leaves. Ramie, like all bast fibers, resists damage by bacteria and fungus, but unlike many bast fibers, it is toxic to numerous bacteria, including staphylococcus and coliform.

Ramie has been cultivated in China, which exports 90 percent of the commercially produced ramie, for more than 5,000 years. Ramie, called *choma* in Japan, was one of the most common fibers used in early Japanese textiles. It is also known as rhea and China Grass. Ramie was used in early Egyptian burial cloth as well.

Ramie is harvested differently from other bast fibers. The plant stems are cut, and the bark is separated from the bast fibers by mechanical scraping and pounding. Ramie is astonishingly white and shiny in its natural state; it is often mistaken for bombyx silk. It accepts dye better than most bast fibers, and it is three times more porous than cotton, making it breathe better than many fibers. Ramie can be spun into an incredibly fine thread and woven into a transparent fabric. Blended with fibers such as cotton, wool, and silk, it makes a beautiful knitting yarn.

ramie

ramie

Seed-Hair Fibers

The other traditional source for textile cellulose is the fiber that protects the seeds of plants. In some cases, such as thistle and milkweed, seed hair helps in seed dispersal, acting like a tiny parachute to carry seeds away from the parent plant. In some plants, like arctic cottons and bear grass, it insulates the seed, keeping it warm as it matures. Although we have spun many different types of seed hair over the centuries—cottonwood, fireweed, milkweed, kapok, arctic cotton—only the seed hair from cotton has survived into modern times as a commercial source of fiber. Cotton, the backbone of the textile world, is produced worldwide. More textiles are made from cotton than from any other single fiber.

cotton flower

COTTON

Cotton comes from a number of trees, shrubs, and herbs all belonging to the *Malvaceae* (mallow) family. It's a close relative of both the hollyhock and hibiscus, having similar flowers and flower bracts. The cotton that we cultivate today is a shrub with dark-green leaves and beautiful flowers. Around each flower are three or four heart-shaped bracts, which remain after the flower head falls off. They contract to hold the seed and the seed hair in place, forming a cotton boll. Inside the cotton boll, the seed-hair fibers surround the seed.

These bundles of fiber are tightly coiled, like little springs, with as many as two to three hundred twists per inch, and the twist alternates direction every three or four turns. The fibers are hollow tubes filled with moisture before the plant ripens. Each day the cotton matures, another layer of cellulose is produced on the inside of the tubes. Layer after layer of cellulose builds up, each one adding to the strength of the fiber, until the core is nearly filled.

These fiber coils, some thirty layers deep, begin to relax and straighten as the seeds ripen, forcing the boll to spring open. As the fibers are released, the water-filled central channel of each fiber is exposed to dry air and sunlight. The fibers dry and flatten, becoming more like ribbons than tubes.

Cotton is a tropical plant that needs plenty of water and heat to grow. Although it is a perennial, it is grown commercially as an annual. Cotton is highly prone to

cotton bolls

cellulose

19

The Organic Movement in Cotton

There has been a great deal of recent interest, from both a social and economic perspective, in developing sustainable organic cotton. One of the movement's most interesting aspects is the cultivation of naturally colored cottons. Colored cottons were once common throughout the world, but their shorter, weaker fibers couldn't be easily processed by machine. The pioneer in this field, Sally Fox, spent years breeding cotton for a longer and stronger staple as well as color and pest resistance. She has registered several genetic patents on naturally colored cottons.

These varieties not only come in an exquisite range of colors, but many also show a resistance to pests and diseases, making them excellent choices for organic agriculture. Although colored cotton has become popular for textile artists, Fox has faced pressure from mainstream cotton producers—even in areas where cotton is grown only as an annual—who fear that her naturally colored genetic lines will contaminate their crops.

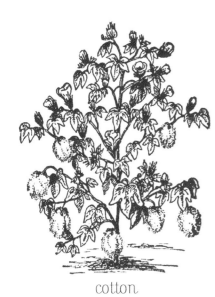

cotton

disease and insect damage, making it one of the highest consumers of pesticides in agriculture worldwide. Using controversial genetic modification, cotton producers have recently been able to reduce the amount of pesticide they use by up to 60 percent by stimulating the plant to produce a protein that's toxic to a number of pests. Cotton crops can also be damaged by rain because cotton fibers are extremely susceptible to mildew.

PROCESSING COTTON

Cotton growers test the cotton daily to see when it is the right time to begin the harvest—too early, the cotton fibers will be weak; too late, the fibers can become brittle. One way to speed up the ripening is to remove the leaves. The plant, which in nature is a perennial, sees this as a death threat and forces all its nutrients into the seeds to ensure the survival of its genes. In northern cotton-growing areas, this defoliation occurs naturally with the first killing frost, but in many areas in the United States, cotton growers use herbicides to remove the leaves. Like the pesticides used in cotton production, the amount of herbicides used is a growing environmental concern.

Once the leaves are removed, the cotton is harvested, either by hand or mechanically. Machines can pick the bolls intact off the plant or harvest only the fiber and the seeds. Either way, cotton is a very efficient source of cellulose—90 percent of the boll is pure cellulose.

After the bolls are harvested, they are *ginned* to separate the fiber from the seeds and any remaining parts of the boll. The cotton gin, famously developed by Eli Whitney in 1793, made the modern cotton industry possible. Before this invention, the cotton fiber was separated by hand from the seeds. Today, a process removes even the *lintners*, the fine, short fibers that coat the seeds and are used primarily to make paper.

eli whitney 1793
invented the cotton gin, automating cotton separation

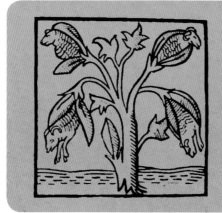

Medieval writer John Mandeville described cotton thus: "There grew there [in India] a wonderful tree which bore tiny lambs on the endes of its branches. These branches were so pliable that they bent down to allow the lambs to feed when they are hungrie."

I learned to spin cotton from the seed from Persis Grayson, who said it was the best way to spin cotton. Just pull gently, straightening the fibers and fanning them out into a fine halo around the seed. Hold the seed with your thumb and finger, rotating it as you spin. The fiber is perfect, not damaged or disordered by processing. It pulls off easily and spins the finest thread effortlessly.

After the fiber is separated from the seeds, it is carded to open up and even out the fibers as well as to remove any remaining vegetable debris. Many yarns are spun from carded cotton, called *sliver*, but high-quality cotton is also combed into top to eliminate the shorter fibers and align them nearly parallel. To make superfine cotton threads, fibers are often combed and recombed several times.

Cotton is also processed by mercerizing. In 1844, working in England, John Mercer discovered that cotton fibers both straightened and became round (rather than ribbonlike) when exposed to caustic soda. Forty years later, Horace Lowe improved the process when he discovered that applying caustic soda to fiber under tension produced incredible luster. Mercerizing strengthens cotton fibers and exposes more dye sites. These additional dye sites and the lustrous surface produce cotton in rich, glowing colors.

THE GLOBAL PATH OF COTTON

The history of cotton is mysterious, but it includes three distinct indigenous sources: India, Africa, and the Americas. Cotton from India spread quickly west into Arabia, then to Egypt and Greece. Pliny described the cotton cloth Egyptian priests used, writing that "no kinds of thread are more brilliantly white or make smoother fabric than this." Cotton moved much more slowly on its eastern journey, reaching China in the thirteenth century as a fiber for paper.

Cotton was introduced to Europe during the Middle Ages, brought back from the Crusades (like so many marvelous things). Accustomed to cloth made from nettle and flax, Europeans were enchanted with cotton's softness, whiteness, and its ability to be spun into extraordinarily fine thread. Because they had no experience with fine, crimpy plant fibers, Europeans first thought that the fiber must come from some unique animal that grew on trees.

In the Americas, samples of both cotton bolls and cloth have been found that are 7,000 years old. When the Spanish came to the Americas and encountered the Pima Indians, they found a cotton-spinning and weaving culture much more sophisticated than any in Europe. Fabrics found in Peru show that cotton was used there long before wool.

All the commercially grown cotton worldwide today comes from the American varietals *Gossypium barbadense* (the long, silky white cotton we know as pima or Egyptian cotton) and *Gossypium hirsutum*. The latter is a successful ancient hybrid of New- and Old-World cotton. Old-World cotton, with thirteen short chromosomes, apparently spread (diffused) to the Americas and bred with the indigenous cotton, which has thirteen long chromosomes, to create twenty-six chromosome cotton. This new cotton hybrid then traveled from the Atlantic Ocean (where Columbus found it in the Bahamas) to the Pacific (where Captain Cook found it in Hawaii). Archeologists are unsure when or how this hybridization happened, but it occurred long before acknowledged contact with the Old World. It is this twice-diffused cotton that is the basis of the giant worldwide cotton industry.

In 1818, the new leader of Egypt, Mohammed Ali Pasha, imported pima cotton seeds from America to replace the weaker and browner cottons originally imported from India, revolutionizing agriculture in Egypt.

In India, Mahatma Gandhi started his Green Revolution by studying the economics of the British cotton trade and the writings of George Washington. Handspinning cotton was central to his nonviolent resistance to British rule. Gandhi was the inspiration for the folding charkha. He said, "India as a nation can live and die only for the spinning wheel."

Gandhi spinning cotton, August 1942.

[CHAPTER TWO]

proteins

Proteins are present in all living structures, from a blade of grass to you and me; they are the workers that make all living things function. The root of the word "protein" comes from the Greek word *prota*, meaning "of primary importance" or "that which comes first."

The two proteins that create the natural fibers for spinning are *keratin*, the substance of hair and wool, and *fibroin*, the structural protein component of silk. Wool and silk have been renewable resources for thousands of years. These fibers have both the strength and structural resilience necessary to wear well. Of the fibers used today, they are the easiest to dye with nature-based or synthetic dyes. Both fibers are easily produced without chemicals and have modest energy requirements. (Regenerated protein fibers from animal and vegetable sources are discussed in Chapter 3.)

PETER AUSTIN

dual-coated
icelandic wool

Keratin Fibers: Wool and Hair

Keratin is the protein that forms the structure of wool, hair, horns and hooves, feathers and quills. Over the last twenty thousand years, we have spun a wide variety of fibers made from this protein. Surprising examples include antelope, ibex, mountain goat, cow, horse, chinchilla, mink, fox, raccoon, and beaver. Historically and in common usage, the terms "hair" and "wool" have been used interchangably. In fiber science, however, the difference between the two is well defined: wool fibers are solid; hair is *medullated*, which means it has a hollow core. The type of hair fiber the follicles produce depends on how wide the medulla is. As the size of the core increases, fibers range from the finest alpaca and Angora rabbit fibers to coarse fibers like kemp and bristle. Medullated fibers tend to accept dye less easily than wool fibers.

WOOL AND HAIR GROWTH

Like human hair, wool grows from a follicle, a tiny tube in the surface of the skin. Wool-bearing animals generally have two types of follicles: primary follicles formed in utero and secondary follicles developed after birth. All the important characteristics of wool are formed here. Crimp develops as the wool cells are forced up the tube toward the surface of the skin. During the passage up the follicle, some cells become harder and some become softer. The harder cells fold the softer cells over, creating a ripple that will be a visible crimp when the new fiber emerges from the skin. Crimp is unique to wool fibers and is what gives wool its amazing resilience. Wool scale, the quality that allows wool to felt, is also formed in the follicle; cells against the outside of the tube become flattened and form the scales and cuticle, cells on the inside elongate and form the cortex. Inside the follicle is also where the difference between wool and hair is established: during the passage through the follicle some fibers develop a medulla (hollow center); other fibers remain solid.

SHEEP'S WOOL

Wool from sheep has been one of the most important textile fibers for nearly 10,000 years. It can be easily grown, gathered, and processed into an extraordinary variety of textiles—from sails to fine underwear. Wool can be made into fabric using every possible textile technique: felting, weaving, knitting, crochet, tatting. It takes dyes easily and wears well.

Wool is easy to produce in a variety of climates and landscapes. Sheep are niche animals, adapting to the conditions in which they live, as does their fleece. North Ronaldsay sheep on the coast of Scotland have adapted successfully to a diet of seaweed. Given the hundreds of different sheep breeds today, the number of possible crossbreeds is hard to imagine. Some breeds, such as Debouillet and Rambouillet, produce excellent wool in semidesert areas that can't support other agricultural

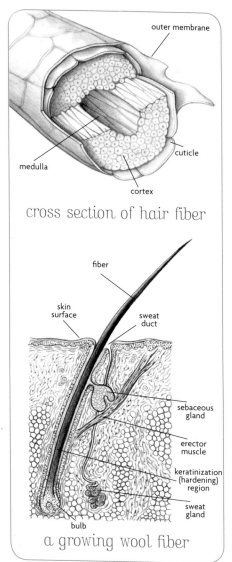

cross section of hair fiber

outer membrane
cuticle
cortex
medulla

a growing wool fiber

fiber
skin surface
sweat duct
sebaceous gland
erector muscle
keratinization (hardening) region
sweat gland
bulb

crops, including breeds of sheep raised primarily for meat.

Some of wool's survival into modern times must be linked with the role that sheep have played in human history. Humans and sheep have traveled the earth together for thousands of years. These hardy animals produced everything humans needed: fleeces for clothing, tents, and blankets for protection from the elements; milk, meat, and blood for food; leather, bone, and sinew for making tools. Their skins were used to record our history—the Dead Sea Scrolls are written on parchment made from sheepskin. Their skins also carried water, oil, and wine. Sheep have been so valuable to us that many cultures used them as a religious sacrifice.

Sheep are prime candidates for negotiating domestication. They are migratory, curious, and adaptable, as opposed to territorial, suspicious, and conservative. Anyone who owns sheep will tell you that their nature is to be interested in what we do. They like us and they rely on us.

SHEDDING AND SHEARING
Before domestication, sheep shed their fleece over spring, summer, and early fall months. By the Bronze Age, sheep were selectively bred to shed their fleece all at once during the late spring. Double-coated Bronze-Age sheep often shed the inner coat first and the outer coat later. When it was time for them to shed, sheep would be brought in to gathering pens and laid down with their legs tied. Spinners combed out the loosening undercoat with their fingers or wooden combs in a process called *rooing*. (Traditionally, the term referred to the collection of the fibers, but it has come to mean the shedding process.) This method is still used in many parts of the world.

Iron-Age developments such as dyepots and wool shears led to fleeces changing again. Fleeces became primarily white for better color when dyed. They also ceased to shed because with the development of shears, natural shedding was no longer efficient. Sheep were also bred for a single coat so that the fleeces were more consistent and did not have to be dehaired before spinning.

Examining cloth samples from the beginning of the Iron Age, archaeologists first thought sheep's wool had been supplemented by wild deer and elk fiber. However, they later realized that the invention of shears meant that all coats of the sheep were removed at once and incorporated into the fabric. Centuries later, when spinners developed tools to separate the coats, the coarser fibers disappeared from the cloth samples.

The ability to shed their fleece (called discontinuous growth factor) to produce multiple coats as well as the ability to produce colored fleece are genetic traits that still exist in modern sheep. When a sheep breed is described as "improved," it means these genes have been suppressed. Improved sheep have a white coat, are even in staple type from tip to tail, and their fleece grows

JUDITH MacKENZIE McCUIN

historic evidence of domestication

Like most domestic animals, sheep were domesticated in the Middle Stone Age, long before written records. The illustrations and records of sheep that started to appear about 3,000 B.C. are about halfway between the beginnings of domestication and sheep today. Sheep have probably been domesticated for 5,500 years, or about 2,000 generations. Wool material was found in the Swiss Lake Dwellings from the Neolithic period (10,000 to 20,000 years ago). Egyptian pictures portraying domestic sheep date back 6,000 years, and a statue of a fully wooled sheep found in a dig in Iran is from the same time period.

By the time of the Babylonian empire—Babylonia means "land of sheep"—3,000 to 4,000 years ago, wool clothing appears to have been relatively common. It appears from the carvings that their sheep were much like sheep today. All sheep come from the area of present-day Afghanistan, Iraq, and Iran, spreading out to other parts of the world. This dispersion includes the Rocky Mountain Bighorn Sheep that, along with bison, walked across the land bridge between Russia and Alaska some 600,000 years ago.

protein

27

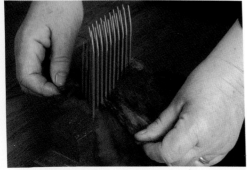

carding and combing

Wool is processed by carding (top) and combing (bottom).

continuously. These traits—color, discontinuous growth, and more than one type of fiber—are now genetically linked. Color can be an indication of the presence of other undesirable traits. (This does not mean that raising colored sheep is bad breeding; it means that beautiful colored fleeces are the result of extraordinarily hard work to make sure that undesirable traits have not been brought forward along with the genes for color.) The ability to take dye well is another trait of improved fiber.

Classing

After wool is shorn from the sheep, it is sorted by quality. (All colored wool is handled separately.) First the fleece is skirted: all the short and dirty fibers around the edge of the fleece are removed along with any "dags" (locks containing manure and dirt). The belly wool, which tends to be uneven in length and overly elastic, is removed along with neck and leg wool, which is shorter and sometimes contains hairy and kempy fibers. The wool is judged by its cleanliness, strength, length, type of white (not all whites are the same), and fineness. Wool is grouped by diameter (micron) and crimp type.

Washing and Scouring

Whether in a commercial mill or at home, wool must be washed or scoured before it can be processed efficiently.

To wash wool without removing its natural oils, just soak it in cold water. Do-

ing so activates the natural detergent qualities of the *suint* (a naturally water-soluble wool oil), which is then removed along with most of the dirt during the rinsing. The wool retains the lanolin and other oils and waxes. This method was traditionally used to produce an "oiled" wool yarn that would be more water resistant for outdoor wear, as in fishermen's ganseys.

Scouring is a more complete washing method that uses heat and detergent to remove all waxes, oil, and suint. Wool must be scoured before dyeing, and many spinners prefer to spin scoured fleece. For wool that that will be combed traditionally, the locks must be kept in order during scouring and often have oil added to them during the combing process.

Carding and Combing

The next step toward making yarn from wool is to card it. The individual wool fibers are loosened from the locks and opened up. Cards are used to brush the locks, which distributes the fibers evenly. In industry, carded fiber can then be put through another process called combing. Traditionally, handspinners comb the fleece after it is washed but while still in lock formation, a perfect preparation for spinning worsted. (See pages 65–68 for more on combing and page 72 on carding.)

Combing removes all the weak, short fibers and aligns the fibers parallel to one another, creating top. In commercial processing, the top is then compressed and steamed to make sure the fibers stay in place until they reach the spinning stage. Wool that has already been carded can still be combed; I have found that combing roving that doesn't spin well often improves the fiber and is well worth any loss of the damaged fibers that the combs remove.

Wool Treatments

Wool can be treated to change its color, strength, and hand. Bleaching removes wool stains and whitens the wool's natural ivory color. The resulting more blue-white fiber lets the wool be dyed brighter colors. Depigmentation uses an enzyme to remove the outer coating of the wool fiber. It does less damage to the fibers than bleaching and essentially produces the same effect as shrink-resistance treatments.

Developed in the 1800s, shrink-resistance treatments allow wool to be machine washed and dried. Much like the mercerizing process for cotton, which uses caustic soda, the shrink-resistant process for wool fiber uses chlorine gas to remove scales and outer cuticle and expose the cortex. With the scales removed, the fibers no longer interlock and cannot felt. One of the side effects of using this method on wool is that it becomes strong and silky, but it loses some of its thermal qualities. The process removes any natural color. However, the treated wool accepts dyes better, producing brilliant colors. An alternate method to prevent shrinking and felting involves coating the fiber with synthetic resins. A

mohair or angora goat

DANIEL MAR

new treatment for wool fiber, marketed under the trade name Optim, removes the scale and stretches the wool permanently so it becomes finer, longer, and silkier.

GOAT FIBERS

Like the use of wool from sheep, the use of goat fibers goes back to pre-history. Domesticated from the wild goats of the Himalayas some 9,000 years ago, goats developed in the same general area of Asia Minor as sheep and spread in similar patterns.

Goats produce different fibers for spinning. In many countries, hair from a wide variety of goats is used to make ropes, tents, and rugs. It makes wonderful rug warp. Mohair, the silky, lustrous fiber of Angora goats, is used in carpets, upholstery, clothing—especially coats and suits—and knitting yarns. Cashmere, a fiber that comes

from several different goats, is one of the true luxury fibers and is used to produce both weaving and knitting yarns.

Mohair

Mohair is produced by the goat called Angora. Recently this goat's name was officially changed to mohair to reduce confusion with Angora rabbit fiber, but both names are still in common use. The name Angora comes from Ankara, the area in Turkey where the goat, like the Angora rabbit and the Angora cat, was developed as a breed.

The story of how this beautiful goat came to Turkey is a well-loved folktale. Suliman Shah, retreating from Genghis Khan, brought the goats with him from the Himalayas. Sequestered in Turkey, the breed was protected and not allowed

protein

29

Mohair is lustrous and accepts dyes beautifully.

to be exported, its fiber used only for royal textiles. Goats were brought back to France during the Crusades, and several brief and unsuccessful efforts to raise them in France followed.

In 1848, the people of Turkey made a gift to the United States of mohair goat breeding stock. The goats have done well in the dry desert lands of Texas and New Mexico, a climate very similar to that of Turkey. South Africa is currently the largest producer of mohair. The United States is the second largest producer, with Texas producing by far the largest percent. Turkey is the third largest.

An important fiber in the Middle East, mohair is used to make a fine cloth that drapes beautifully and dyes like a jewel. Mohair is also used for knotted pile carpets. It is perfect for this type of construction; it has no crimp, so it opens readily once the knots are tied and cut. Because mohair largely lacks the scale structure found in wool, its smooth surface reflects light, making it incredibly lustrous. It is the strongest of all the keratin fibers and can withstand the rugged use that a carpet receives.

In the modern world, mohair has been used to make a wide range of textiles, from velvet-pile upholstery and tuxedoes to filmy shawls and sweaters. In the 1960s, spinning mills developed a method to produce a looped mohair yarn that is soft and airy when brushed. Mohair found a whole new focus as a fashion fiber.

Mohair develops in much the same way as wool in the follicle, but both the primary and secondary follicles produce the same fiber—there is no second coat. The fiber is long and straight, uncrimped but wavy. Sometimes locks form ringlets, a good sign of fineness in the fleece, which should be free of coarse medullated fibers. Mohair grows continuously and does not shed naturally in a healthy animal. It is shorn twice a year, in the spring and fall, with the fall clip being the choice one. Although the term "kid" refers to a baby goat, it also indicates the degree of fineness; a ten-year-old goat can produce kid mohair.

Traditionally, mohair goats are white. However, breeders of naturally colored mohair goats have recently formed a registry, and the popular colored goats now come in a lovely range of browns, reds, blacks, and grays.

Cashmere

For centuries, cashmere has been the fiber of luxury and elegance. Its characteristics of warmth without weight, exquisite draping, and incomparable hand have made it the favorite of textile designers everywhere. Since the introduction of cashmere to Europe in the eighteenth century, cashmere's popularity has never waned. Cashmere is the only commercial fiber for which demand exceeds supply.

The original source for cashmere, the goat *Capra hircus laniger*, is a close relative of the Angora goat and thrives on the arid, sparse shoulders of the Himalayas. Unlike Angora goats, cashmere goats have a double-coated fleece. Ideally, the hair-and-bristle outer coat is quite a bit coarser than the inner coat; the bigger the difference between the diameters of the two coats, the easier it is to dehair the fiber. Goats develop an undercoat—the fiber from the secondary follicles—to protect themselves from the extreme winters of these mountainous regions. It is shed naturally as the weather becomes warm again.

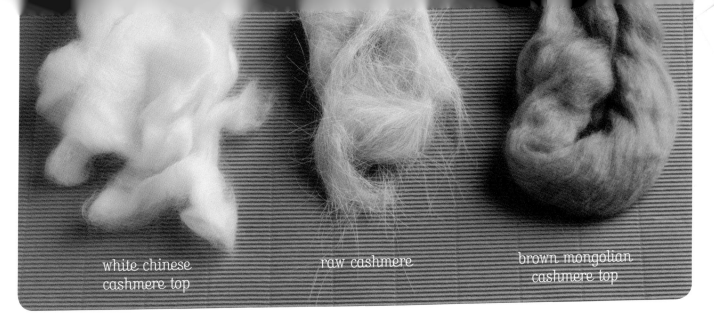

white chinese cashmere top

raw cashmere

brown mongolian cashmere top

Unlike many fibers, cashmere is not defined by the breed of animal it is harvested from. Cashmere is a type of fiber, not just a particular breed of goat. Although some types of goats produce better cashmere fiber more abundantly than others, no one genetic breed solely produces cashmere fiber. Until December 2006, when a law was passed to bring the U.S. definitions in line with world standards, fiber labeled as cashmere in the United States didn't have to come from a goat—as long as it met the legal description of the fiber, it could come from a hamster!

In the United States, the current legal definition of cashmere is the undercoat fiber from a goat; the fiber must have a micron count of 19 or finer, with less than 3 percent by weight of the fibers exceeding 30 microns. It must be at least 1¼ inches (3 centimeters) long. But cashmere classers look for one more important trait: character. Character refers to the type of crimp structure. In the case of cashmere, the proper character is a "deeply lobed crimp," meaning that the crimp is as wide as the unextended fiber is tall. Fibers, even those from a "cashmere" goat, that meet all the criteria of fineness and micron deviation but lack the crimp structure of cashmere will be classed as "not quite cashmere" or cashgora.

Character is what makes cashmere so springy and able to hold its shape. It is also what makes it incredibly warm and lightweight, because the crimp maintains lots of air pockets. Cashmere is not lustrous; fabric made from it should have a velvety, light-absorbing surface because the crimp refracts light in many directions. The crimp structure and lack of well-defined scales makes cashmere harder to felt; it tends to full or expand when agitated with soap and hot water. The soft hand of cashmere comes from that scale structure; although the scales exist, they are elongated, very smooth, and almost indiscernible.

Cashmere is collected in several different ways: as in Kashmir, from rocks and bushes in areas where the goats shed; as in much of Mongolia, by combing out the undercoat as the goats begin their annual molt; or as

cashmere goat

ANNE MERROW

protien

31

 is labeled with vertical text "LISA ROSKOPF"

pygora goat

Pygora

The fiber from this unusual goat, though not yet truly commercial, is gaining a following among handspinners, especially those who want to raise a fiber-producing animal in a small space.

Pygoras were developed in Oregon in the 1970s by crossing an African pygmy goat buck with an Angora goat doe in an effort to produce colored mohair. The goats that resulted from this cross were surprising. They were not only colored but had one of three different fleece types: a very fine, silky, often colored mohair-type coat that didn't coarsen with age (type A); a true cashmere coat (type C); and a coat that was a combination of the other two, 3 to 6 inches (7.5 to 15 centimeters) long with some wavy crimp (type B). All three coats have varying amounts of coarse bristly fiber that must be removed by dehairing. Usually, Pygoras are shorn if they have type A and B coats and either combed or shorn if they have type C coats.

Raised primarily for fiber, the animals have another plus: the cute factor. They are fairly small and dainty—18 to 23 inches (46 to 58.5 centimeters) tall—and covered with silky ringlets. Their appealing looks and friendly nature make them wonderful pets.

in China, Australia, and the United States, where it is sheared off, which removes both the hairy outer coat and the downy undercoat.

However cashmere fiber is collected, it must be dehaired after the sorted fibers are washed and dried. Although dehairing can be done by hand, it is slow, labor-intensive work. Machines simplify the process. Dehairing machines resemble carding machines; as the fiber passes through the series of rollers, the fine fibers stay on the drums and the coarser fibers fall into bins below. Aside from dehairing, cashmere is processed much like wool—the fiber is either carded or made into top in preparation for spinning. Cashmere comes in a wide range of natural colors, but bright white is the most sought-after because it's generally finer and can be dyed brilliant colors.

a caravanserai

CAMELIDS

Camelids are a large and ancient group of animals found in both the Old and New Worlds. The group includes camels, alpacas, llamas, vicuñas, and guanacos. All camelids originate in North America—there are camel fossil remains in Montana—although the indigenous North American camelids became extinct by the last Ice Age. Early camelids split into two groups, the camels moving north along the narrow grasslands at the edge of the ice fields 600,000 years ago and crossing through Beringia (now the Bering Sea) into Asia. The second group, vicuñas and guanacos, moved south to spread into parts of South America, particularly along the spine of the Andes. No evidence explains why some North American camelids drifted south from their origins in the North American grasslands and others moved north into Northern Asia and Africa.

Old World Camelids

There are two types of camels, the dromedary (one hump) and the Bactrian (two humps). These animals have spread throughout Asia and Africa, becoming beasts of burden and suppliers of food, providing both milk and meat. They also provide leather, hair (used for cords, ropes, tents, and the warp of Persian carpets), and a softer undercoat (used for clothing and blankets). Although both types of camels produce fiber, the fiber used in the textile world comes from Bactrian camels, which produce significantly more and better quality fiber than dromedaries. Dromedaries are true desert dwellers, living predominantly in Western Asia and North Africa. Bactrians are hardy cold-weather animals found in the north of central Asia, in Tibet, Afghanistan, and the Gobi Desert.

Camels can survive in amazingly hostile conditions, but they still became nearly extinct in the wild in most areas by 3,000 B.C. Today, only the Gobi Desert in Mongolia has a small population—two to three hundred—that are considered wild. Australia imported camels in 1840 to help open up the arid lands of Western Australia; they were used until the early 1900s. The Australian climate seems to have agreed with camels; there are now about 700,000 feral camels that inhabit the continent.

Camels play another role in the fiber world: It is on their backs that silk was brought to the West. The silk routes from China and Iran to Turkey used camels. The old caravanserais in Turkey are spaced 26 miles apart—the distance a fully loaded camel could travel in a day. Even though the camels have long since been replaced by trucks, you

bactrian camels

33

camel yarn

1. dromedary
2. bactrian

can still smell their distinctive odor blended with cookfire smoke and boiled tea in the old buildings on the silk route.

Camels have several distinct coats: an outer hair coat that is mostly straight and coarse, as long as 15 inches (38 centimeters); a middle coat with a texture similar to a fine sheep's wool, usually 3 to 5 inches (7.5 to 12.5 centimeters); and a soft, springy inner coat similar to cashmere, but less fine, 1 to 3 inches (2.7 to 7.5 centimeters). Like cashmere, this fine undercoat is collected by combing. The rest of the coat continues to shed after the downy undercoat has broken free in big mats. These mats are collected from the camels or from rocks and bushes.

Camel fiber comes in several distinct colors, from a deep tawny caramel to the palest fawn. Although gray and white camels exist, they are quite rare. Most camel fiber takes color from natural or synthetic dyes reasonably well.

Camel is processed like most natural protein fibers. After it is collected, it is sorted by fiber type and fineness, then washed and dehaired. The long, coarse outer-coat fibers make warp yarns for rugs and woven fabric for tents. The finer outer-coat fibers become camel hair brushes for artists. The middle-coat fibers are used to make yarn for weaving and knitting; the yarn can be fulled and napped to make a dense but lightweight fabric that resists wrinkling. This is the fabric of the classic camel-hair coat. The short undercoat fibers are spun woolen and used primarily for very fine cloth and lace-knitting yarns.

New World Camelids

Evidence of South American camelid domestication starts about 5,000 years ago, and those ancient efforts produced the animals we now know as alpacas and llamas. During the Inca empire, rigorous breeding programs refined llamas into excellent pack and guard animals and alpacas into more than a dozen distinct colors. Although it was once believed that both alpacas and llamas are descended from the guanaco, it is now understood that vicuñas were bred to produce alpacas for fiber and meat and guanacos to produce hardy llamas for transportation. There are no wild alpacas or llamas.

With the Spanish conquest of South America in 1532 and the introduction of sheep, all New-World camelids became endangered. The Spanish brought their own textile culture with them, and alpacas, llamas, vicuñas, and guanacos were all seen as competing for grazing lands. They were hunted, especially vicuñas and guanacos, to near extinction.

Llamas and alpacas can cross breed. If the cross is a llama male and an alpaca female, the offspring is called a *huarizo*; if the cross is an alpaca male and a llama female, the offspring is called a *misti* (paco-llama).

Alpaca

During the time of the Incas, a focused and recorded breeding program was created for alpacas. Animals were raised in separate areas depending on their color. If a rose-colored *cria* (baby) was born in a russet area, it would be moved after weaning to the rose-colored flock. Using this method, the Incas developed more than twenty well-defined natural colors. They also bred for dense, fine, long coats. Most importantly, they bred for a single coat, eliminating the rough outer coat common to camelids.

Alpaca fiber is a hair rather than a true wool. Alpaca fiber's medulla is a series of little air sacs, not unlike bubble wrap. This structure contributes to alpaca's insulating properties, making it both lightweight and warm. The lack of multiple coats and the fineness of the fibers make alpaca silky to the touch and give it an incredible hand. Unlike sheep's wool, alpaca contains little or no fiber oil or wax. Alpaca is classed as a specialty fiber; about 4,000 tons are produced each year, compared to wool's 430,000 tons a year. Alpaca fiber is incredibly strong, at least three times stronger than the strongest wool fiber. It becomes even stronger when wet.

The two distinct types of alpacas are huacaya and suri. Ninety percent of all alpacas are huacaya, but the types are not fully separated—the offspring of two huacayas can be a suri, and vice versa. Although suris are rare, evidence shows that they too were domesticated and that their silky fleece was considered a luxury. Huacayas have a dense, fine, somewhat crimpy coat. Their fleece ranges from 18 to 27 microns. Suris have a very fine, silky coat that is often ringletted. Suri fleece lacks the density and crimp structure of huacaya fleece, but what it lacks in volume is made up for by the silk-like luster of the fine straight fibers. Suri fleece ranges from 10 to 15 microns.

Alpaca fiber is separated during shearing into prime, seconds, and discards. The prime fleece is called a blanket and comes roughly from the area of the animal that would be covered by a saddle blanket. Blankets are further graded by fiber diameter, fiber length, fiber color, cleanliness, and degree of medullation. Seconds include fiber from the shoulders, haunches, and necks; discards include fiber from the legs, tail, and belly, which are coarser and uneven in micron.

Alpaca is used primarily for woven or knitted clothing and fabric. It also makes incredible knotted-pile carpet and velvet material that is stunning to touch and wears surprisingly well.

Llama

Llamas are the largest of the New-World camelids and the largest mammals native to South America. Llamas were used for meat, hides, and wool some 6,000 years ago. It was during the time of the Incas that the llamas we see today were developed. The Incas bred for strength, endurance,

alpaca

and domestication traits—llamas are curious and friendly—to create the perfect pack animal.

Llamas were imported to the United States in the 1970s as backcountry pack animals, and their suitability in the ecology of mountain regions has made them a popular animal in North America. Like all camelids, their two-toed feet are padded, so they don't damage trails. These hardy animals can eat whatever is available along the trail and, being efficient food converters (they are semiruminants), they don't need much to sustain them.

Llamas are double-coated, with clean legs and faces. They have a long, strong outer coat that sheds water and protects them from bad weather and a soft, springy inner coat that keeps them warm in the winter and sheds as the weather becomes warmer. Llamas have medullated fiber that lacks oils and wax and has little odor. I have seen dehaired llama fiber in a wide range of colors that was hard to distinguish from large-diameter cashmere.

alpacas

JARNO GONZALEZ ZARRAONANDIA

protien

35

llama

As llamas have increasingly been used as fiber animals, their fleece has changed. Today, it is not uncommon to see llamas with little of the outer coat that has been a distinguishing characteristic of traditional llama fleece. Some llama fleeces are as dense and wavy as alpaca. In most double-coated animals, the inner coat becomes coarser and sometimes loses its ability to shed when the outer coat disappears, but I have not seen this with the llama.

A new fiber trend is the suri llama. Like suri alpacas, suri llamas have a distinctive fleece that hangs in independent locks. The locks are highly lustrous, dense, and smooth. The traditional llama undercoat is absent. Like suri alpacas, evidence shows that suri llamas existed in limited numbers thousands of years ago.

Vicuña

The smallest of the camelids, vicuñas live on the rugged high grasslands of the Andes. They have adapted to extreme temperatures by developing a dense, fine insulating coat. Their teeth grow constantly, like a rabbit's, so they can chew the tough mountain grasses that make up most of their diet. Their flexible even toes ("ungulate" means even-toed) help them climb rocky slopes.

Vicuñas have been hunted for their meat, hides, and fiber more than 6,000 years. They were not easily domesticated, as their wild, nervous nature made it difficult

paco-vicuña

A new type of alpaca, the paco-vicuña, has recently been recognized. Bred selectively in North America for its amazing fiber, the paco-vicuña seems to bring forward the best of both alpacas and vicuñas. The fiber is longer and denser than that of its wild ancestors but considerably finer than most alpaca fiber. Paco-vicuña fiber is between 12 and 20 microns. Although it lacks the color range of a true alpaca, the warm russet color characteristic of the vicuña is lovely. The fiber is quite soft but contains some guard hair, which must be removed for spinning. Paco-vicuña fiber is harvested every two to three years, rather than yearly for alpaca or every three to four years for vicuña.

It might seem faster to cross an alpaca and a vicuña to get a paco-vicuña, but it would also be illegal. Instead, those who raise them breed together alpacas that exhibit paco-vicuña traits. Vicuñas have been endangered for many years. Recently, their status has been upgraded to threatened as their numbers have improved, but it is currently illegal to own vicuñas or vicuña crosses in North America.

PHIL SWITZER

JOOST DE RAEYMAEKER

guanacos

for them to exist in captivity. When the Incas rounded them up to harvest their fiber, many animals died during the process. Vicuña fiber is incredibly soft and light. The softness and drape of the pelt is simply incomparable. Having held a vicuña pelt in my hands, I am not surprised that these animals were coveted.

In fact, vicuñas were so prized that they were hunted nearly to extinction. By 1960, only 6,000 vicuñas were known to survive. Thankfully, Chile and Peru established national parks to protect them, and many countries, including the United States, banned the import and use of their fiber and pelts. Vicuñas are starting to rebuild their population (125,000 at last count), and a number of them have been raised in captivity. After being banned from sale or possession in North America for many years, vicuña fiber and products made from it are now allowed on the market. However, any vicuña products must have documentation certifying that the source animals are domesticated.

Vicuñas are dual-coated, so the fiber needs to be dehaired before it's ready to spin. It is incredibly fine, with an average micron range of 8 to 13. Vicuña comes in only one color, a beautiful russet. Vicuñas produce a harvestable coat every three to four years.

Guanaco

The guanaco is the largest of the wild New-World camelids; it stands nearly 4 feet (1.4 meters) tall at the shoulder. It is alert, fast, and sure-footed. Although guanacos are very difficult to domesticate, evidence reveals that Bolivian Indians occasionally raised them in captivity when the guanaco population was threatened by starvation, predation, or disease. Guanacos have long been on the endangered species list, but their population is now about 500,000 and their endangered status is listed as "least concern," the lowest of the endangerment categories. For many years, it was illegal to import or sell guanaco fiber, but now

that a number of domesticated herds have been established, a limited amount of the fiber is available for handspinning. Like llamas, guanacos are dual-coated. Their fine undercoat is similar to that of vicuñas, though less fine and sparser.

ANGORA RABBITS

Rabbits are the most recent mammals to have been domesticated. All our domestic rabbits descend from the wild rabbits (*Oryctolagus cuniculus*) that originated in the area that is now Spain. Although rabbits of every kind have been used for their pelts and food for the last 10,000 years, the rabbits used for textiles are a specific breed called Angora. Angora rabbits are a phenotype rather than a distinct species, as are Angora cats, Angora goats, suri llamas, suri alpacas, and paco-vicuñas. A small genetic deviation causes the fiber to grow extra long, fine, and straight. The deviation is often linked with

vicuñas

CHARLES NOVAL

protien

37

TERESA LEVITE

angora rabbit

Angora rabbits produce three types of hair: an undercoat, erector hair, and guard hair. The undercoat is very fine (about 10 microns). The erector hair is rather silky and a bit stiff, and it rises to bring the down coat up with it when the rabbit is cold, much the way human hairs raise in goose bumps. The guard hair, called *awn*, is thin at the bottom (near the skin) and wider at the top; it falls over the soft undercoat to protect it. The erector coat and the guard coat, both longer than the soft undercoat, are the fibers that produce angora's soft, shining halo. Angora fiber comes in a range of soft, natural colors and a stunning blue-white. The fiber is beautiful on its own but also takes dyes well.

Three main types of rabbits produce commercial fiber: English, French, and German. Each produces a slightly different type of hair. English Angora rabbits have the softest coat, with little guard hair and are the most like cashmere. They have woolly ears, faces, and legs, and are a bit harder to maintain. French Angora rabbits have a larger proportion of guard hair and produce the most fur-like fabrics. They are clean-faced, with no hair on their ears or legs, making them much easier to groom. German Angora rabbits are the largest breed, weighing about 15 pounds (6.8 kilograms), and they produce the most fiber. They are always white, and their fiber is coarser than that of the other two but still wonderfully soft and shiny. Although you will see many crossbreeds of all these rabbits, these three are the main fiber producers.

A new breed, Satin, has emerged in the last few years. Although not available in large enough amounts to market commercially, satin fiber is well worth seeking out.

It is similar to German Angora except that the fiber is much more reflective, producing unusually intense colors. Satin fiber comes in a range of colors including true black, cinnamon, and sable.

Angora fiber is harvested in two ways, either plucked as the fiber loosens in its natural shedding cycle or sheared. Hand-plucked prime angora locks laid in perfect order are a joy to spin by hand. The fibers will change slightly if the coat is shorn off the rabbit, as it is in most commercial processes. Commercial blends use angora that has been shorn. Angora blends well with silk and fine wools such as Merino.

Angora rabbit fiber lacks oil and wax and can be spun just as it comes off the rabbit. Although some people are allergic to angora fiber, the allergy is usually a reaction to the rabbit's grooming saliva. If you have a reaction, try washing the fiber before you spin it to see if that corrects the problem.

RARE FIBERS

Rare fibers are not commonly used commercially because they exist in too small an amount to be practical for industry to pursue. Fortunately for handspinners, these fibers are often available to us. Collected in small amounts and varying from year to year, they often differ widely in color and quality. It's a good idea to buy what you think you might need all at one time.

Both yak and bison fibers come primarily from domesticated animals. Most qiviut is obtained from wild musk ox under government control (much like elk and deer), although a few musk ox are kept in captivity. In many countries, including the United States, it's illegal to

a particular white color called bright—a blue-white—and sometimes with true albino features such as red eyes. The use of the word "angora" to describe a fiber always means Angora rabbit fiber.

Angora is one of the most sensuous fibers, combining the hand of cashmere and silk. It is impossible not to touch. Angora fiber has long, smooth, chevron-shaped scales. It is a hair, not a wool. It has a pronounced interrupted medulla, which means that the medulla is bridged at regular intervals. Essentially, angora fiber is a tube of balloons all spaced at regular intervals. These air pockets create thermal insulation without weight, which makes angora one of the lightest, warmest fibers available.

BUFFALOGOLD.NET

bison

raw bison

dehaired bison

dyed bison

possess *shatoosh*, fiber from the *chiru*, the endangered Tibetan antelope. The use of shatoosh is controversial and the cause of much concern amongst conservationists and the worldwide fiber community.

Bison

Bison are the New World's largest land mammals. They came across the land bridge from Siberia some 600,000 years ago—the same route the camels used to migrate to Asia and Africa, in the opposite direction. At one time, bison, woolly mammoths, and musk ox roamed the great interior grasslands from Alaska to Northern Mexico, sometimes in mixed herds. Before European contact, bison herds are estimated to have numbered seventy million. These massive animals have no natural predators—they're fast (much faster than humans), alert, and protective of one another.

But within a few years of the introduction of horses, guns, and trains, the seemingly endless herds were gone, hunted deliberately like the vicuña to near-extinction. Their numbers dropped from millions to less than fifteen hundred. Fortunately, by the 1880s, some people realized what a great tragedy their loss would be, and they

were protected by the U.S. government and private individuals.

Recently, bison have been raised commercially for meat and hides; in combination with the bison refuges in North America, the total number of bison has risen. Today, a little more than a hundred years after their numbers were lowest, the bison population is about 200,000.

Bison fiber is similar to qiviut, yak down, and cashmere, all of which protect the animals from harsh cold. Bison have five distinct fiber types: a long, wiry outer coat that protects the bison from rain, snow, and wind; a medium-length coarse coat that adds structure and air pockets; and three increasingly shorter and softer down undercoats that provide the thermal mass necessary to keep this huge animal warm in a climate of extreme winter temperatures, sometimes as low as minus 60° Fahrenheit (minus 51° Celsius).

Bison shed all of their coats sometime between March and June. The underdown loosens first, then all the fibers come off in huge mats. This shed fiber can be collected, but make sure that there are no bison still in the area before you start collecting fiber—they're fast and give no warning. Fiber can also be collected from the hides of animals

39

yak

that have gone to slaughter. Bison fiber needs to be dehaired, either by hand or commercially, to remove the two rough coats and leave the down. The hair that is separated out makes a wonderful rug yarn. All bison fiber is brown, with some slight variations. Bison down fiber is currently available commercially from several suppliers.

Yak

Yaks come from Central Asia, where they live in the mountainous Himalayan regions, often at altitudes up to 20,000 feet. There are yak herds in China, Tibet, Nepal, and India. Like bison, yaks form the basis of human survival in these areas of extreme weather conditions, providing hair

yak down

for yurts, oil for lamps, clothing, blankets, milk, and meat. Yak fiber is the most readily available of all the rare fibers.

Yaks have been used for centuries for transportation along the mountainous trade routes between China, India, and Tibet. They have been selectively bred to be slightly less wild than bison and musk ox, letting them serve as both pack and riding animals. Yaks that exhibit more docile traits are milked; yak butter, cheese, and oil for cooking form a major part of the diet for people in the Himalayan regions. Because yaks are handled more often than bison and musk ox, people can collect yak down by combing out the animals as they start to shed their undercoat. Violent changes in weather in these wild mountain regions make it dangerous to shear the animals; a yak can survive minus 40° Fahrenheit (minus 40° Celsius) without shelter because of its protective coat.

Yaks come in several types; the Royal Himalayan is the largest and has a striking coat, white with black markings. Black yaks are most common, but you may also find brindled yaks with a mottled coat of brown, gray, and cream. The number of yak herds in North America is growing, especially in the Rocky Mountain areas of both Canada

and the United States, where they are primarily raised as pets and pack animals. However, interest in collecting their fiber is increasing.

The fiber is treated like cashmere: graded by color and quality, then washed, dehaired, and spun. Most yak down is slightly finer than bison, 18 to 21 microns. Depigmented yak fiber is also available for spinners. It has been treated with a process similar to shrink-proofing, which removes the fiber's outer scales and cuticle and makes it white. Depigmented yak has a lovely silky hand and can be dyed brilliant colors, but some of its thermal qualities are lost.

Qiviut

Like bison, musk ox are some of the oldest surviving herbivores on the planet. Musk ox are thought to have originated in the grasslands of Asia, moving with the woolly rhinoceros and caribou into Siberia, across Beringia, and into North America about 200,000 years ago. Their range was vast; they shared grasslands with bison and woolly mammoths as far south as Nebraska and east into Ohio. They spread across the Canadian North and into Greenland. When the ice retreated and the oceans rose, musk ox herds remained in Alaska,

40

the Yukon, the Northwest Territories of Canada, and Greenland.

People of the north have depended on musk ox in the same way that people of the Himalayas have depended on yaks and the Plains people on bison—as their life support. Just as contact with Europeans destroyed the balance between tribal people and the bison, so the introduction of guns and European markets destroyed the balance between the people of the north and the musk ox. The musk ox were relentlessly hunted until the Canadian government banned all musk-ox hunting in 1917, when the musk ox in Canada numbered only 500. Fortunately, once protected from uncontrolled hunting, musk ox have made a strong comeback. Herds have been re-introduced to Alaska, Siberia, Greenland, and the eastern Canadian arctic. According to the U.S. Fish and Wildlife Service, musk ox now number about 125,000, more than half of which are in Canada.

Musk ox is one of the the rarest legally available fibers. It is also the finest, warmest, and lightest natural fiber. Like bison, musk ox have five distinct types of fiber. In June and July the musk ox "blow" their undercoats; the down fibers not needed in the warmer temperatures are released from the skin in clumps. The clumps blow across the bushes and grasses of the tundra. The down, called qiviut, can be collected from the ground or collected from hides; it must be gathered and dehaired like bison, yak, and cashmere.

Tibetan Antelope

The Tibetan antelope is native to the Tibetan plateau region, where it lives in large migratory herds similar to North American antelope. Its Tibetan name is *chiru* and it is the source of a much sought-after fiber called *shatoosh* (also *shahtoosh or shatush*), a word that means "king's wool." To harvest the fiber, the animal is killed. One chiru will yield about 3.5 to 4 ounces (100 to 113 grams) of fiber. Shatoosh has been used for making the finest shawls imaginable—truly "woven wind." These shawls, similar to Kashmiri shawls, were richly embroidered and were the gifts of kings.

The fiber is brought from Tibet and Nepal to be woven in the province of Kashmir. Because of their rarity and beauty, the shawls have become a desired symbol of affluence. The unlimited hunting to acquire this lucrative fiber has led in recent years to as many as 20,000 antelopes being shot per year. Many countries, including China, India, and the United States, have made possessing of shatoosh shawls illegal in an effort to protect these endangered animals.

qiviut (musk ox)

JOHN FUGETT

protien

Fibroin Fiber: Silk

Is there any other fiber whose very name implies luxury and sensuality, affluence and romance? Silk is often used as a comparative word—silken skin and silken tresses, a sailor's sea as smooth as silk, a wind as soft as silk—because nothing else is quite like it.

Almost every country has some kind of silk-producing insect; spiders, ants, and moths can all produce silk. Silk can even be produced by marine life. Plentiful evidence shows that silk from a variety of wild silkworms was used in the Mediterranean areas long before the introduction of silk from China during Roman times. But Chinese sericulture—the cultivation and reeling of silkworms—changed the definition of what silk could be. Finer, longer, stronger, much more lustrous, and stunningly white, silk fiber captivated and revolutionized the textile world.

China tried to protect its monopoly on silk and succeeded for nearly two thousand years. But a Chinese princess smuggled the eggs of the silk moth and the seeds of the mulberry tree to Khotan in A.D. 419 in her headdress. Silk culture spread quickly from there to Persia. Nestorian monks smuggled silkworms and mulberry seeds into Constantinople, where the Byzantium Empire also tried in vain to keep it secret. From there, the cultivation spread around the Mediterranean and, with the Moorish invasion of Spain, into Europe.

Silk is classified as either cultivated, meaning bombyx, or tussah. Bombyx comes from several different but closely related moths. The one most commonly used for modern silk production is *Bombyx mori*. The filament has no pigment and is

silk cocoons

a brilliant blue-white. The worm is fairly "host specific"—without white mulberry leaves, it has difficulty surviving. Domesticated for thousands of years, it depends on human cultivation for its survival. Japan, China, France, Italy, the Philippines, Thailand, and India are all producers of bombyx silk.

Tussah originally referred to a type of silk from India from the *Anthera mylitta* moth; now it commonly means any silk that isn't bombyx. Tussah silkworms are found in nearly every part of the world. Their silk varies widely in quality, amount, and color, as does whether they can be raised in captivity. Tussah is sometimes referred to as "wild" silk, which implies that it isn't raised and comes only from hatched-out cocoons gathered in the wild. In fact, tussah can be and is raised commercially, just like bombyx silk.

Tussah moths are harder to raise than Bombyx moths, which have been selected for thousands of years for domestication. Tussah cocoons are also collected in many areas before the moth hatches and pierces the cocoon. But a percentage of tussah silk, especially from artisan silk co-ops, does come from pierced cocoons collected in

the wild. Tussah cocoons are much larger than Bombyx cocoons, and the silk is not as fine or lustrous. Tussah comes in a range of colors from a pale cream to a rich dark brown; it's never the blue-white color of bombyx.

Silkworms have a fascinating life cycle. The eggs (called *graine*) are tiny, as small as the head of a pin, but so strong you could stand on them without breaking them. Like those of all moths, the eggs can withstand extremes in temperature; normal freezing won't kill them, and they can withstand temperatures above 100° Fahrenheit (38° Celsius). They can remain dormant for long periods of time until conditions are right for them to hatch.

When the eggs hatch, the worms immediately start to eat and continue to do so for the next three to five weeks. They weigh 10,000 times more at the end of their eating cycle and shed their skin, including their jawbones, five times during this period. At the end of the eating cycle, the silk gland becomes enormous, about 50 percent of the weight of the worm.

When they are ready to spin their cocoon, the worms find a place to anchor themselves. They secrete fibroin as a liquid

tussah silk

from two ducts called spinnerets under the silkworm's lower lip. As the two streams of fibroin hit the air, they harden and are "glued" together by another protein called sericin, which in turn hardens to form the rigid cocoon. During this chrysalis state, the worm starts the miraculous process of turning into a moth. Depending on the type of moth, it may take a month or years to go through this transformation. When the metamorphosis is complete, the moth releases moisture to dissolve the end of the cocoon. The moth literally drools its way out, although the act is called piercing. It struggles out of its cocoon, stretches and dries its wings, and it's ready to fly, mate, and lay eggs to start the next cycle—all in the course of its two- or three-day life.

Reeling

Silk is unique in the textile world: it's the only natural fiber that isn't spun to make a thread. The finest quality silks, called reeled silks, are used just as they're wound off the cocoon. Although bombyx silk can be reeled easily because it has been bred for a dense, compact cocoon, many tussah silks can be reeled as well.

To make reeled silk, the chrysalises are stifled in an oven or placed in an extremely hot room several days after the cocoons are spun. Once the chrysalises are dead, the cocoons are sorted by size and shape and any that are stained are removed. The perfect cocoons are placed in very hot water to soften and dissolve the sericin (which

is water soluble) and release the fibroin (which is not). The middle coat of the cocoon is the part that is reeled; the coarse, uneven outer coat (the first spinning) is slipped off and set aside, as is the inner part of the cocoon, which is very fine and weak. Silk is usually reeled from several cocoons at once, and cocoons are replaced as they run out. A good reeler must be able to keep the diameter the same throughout the skein, just as a good handspinner must be able to maintain an even diameter throughout a bobbin. Except for another wash or two, the silk is now ready to be used.

It can also be made into silk thread or yarn by being "thrown," or having twist added to it. Throwing comes from the Anglo Saxon word "thrawn," meaning "to twist," and is a different process from spinning because there is no drafting of fiber.

Recently, North America has experienced a great revival of interest in raising silkworms, both imported and native species. Many people have learned to harvest their silkworms and reel their own silk.

Cocoons that aren't of good enough quality to be reeled can be degummed in the cocoon stage, carded, and then put through the top-making process. The fiber is sold for spinning as silk top or silk brick. The noils, or broken short fibers, are what is left in the teeth of the carder. Noil can be spun using the same spinning methods as for cotton. It makes a soft nubbly yarn that has many of the attributes of silk, just not the luster or the strength.

bombyx silk

Michael Cook reels silk from silkworms he cultivated.

MICHAEL COOK

MICHAEL COOK

bombyx moth

variety of luxury fibers. Some surprisingly successful silk blends include cotton, hemp, and linen. One of the most wearable fabrics is 50/50 cotton/silk, especially for traveling because it's indestructible, doesn't crease, and feels comfortable in any climate.

Spinners can also buy silk in cocoons, hankies, or caps. Hankies and caps are comprised of layered cocoons that have been boiled to remove the sericin. The cocoons are then opened up, the worm parts are removed, and the cocoons are stretched one on top of the other on a frame to dry.

Silk is available blended with a wide

SPIDER SILK

Spider silk is composed of fibroin, just like the silk from silkworms and fan mussels. Young spiders produce gossamer, a fine balloon silk, to carry them away from their nests. Human use of spider silk has a long and interesting history. The people of England gave Eleanor of Aquitaine a gos-

spider silk

samer shawl as a wedding present when she married Henry II. In the 1950s, a group in France supported its commune by weaving and selling spider silk ties and shirts.

Spiders are really little silk factories, able to produce as many as five quite different types of silk for different purposes. Spider silk is the strongest and finest natural fiber, averaging 2.5 to 3 microns. It has natural antibiotic and antifungal properties and has been used in medicine even in modern times. It's also used in scopes, sights, and fine scientific instruments.

Because it has so many uses, science and industry have tried many times to mimic the structure of spider silk synthetically. Recently, a research group in Canada did a transgenetic experiment to see if spider silk genes could be introduced in dairy goats. The resulting goat milk contained a high amount of fibroin. Unfortunately, humans still have a few tricks to learn; although we can make the milk, we still can't spin the silk.

To collect spider silk, look for the spiders' raceways, the long, silky strands they use to get to their webs. (Web silk is one of the other five threads spiders make; the web-silk strands are sticky to hold the spiders' prey and aren't used for spinning.) You can collect strands of raceway silks by "reeling" them around several cardboard tubes or weaving bobbins. Then become a silk throwster and ply them together.

BYSSUS: SILK OF THE SEA

Some years ago, I saw a beautiful little bag in a lace museum in France that looked for all the world as if it had been made from gold thread. When I read "mussel" in the museum description, I thought it was simply my inadequate French, but it was indeed spun from filaments made from fibroin and extruded through the spinnerets of a mussel. The name of the fiber is *tarentine*, and it's said to have made gloves so fine they could be folded into a walnut shell.

The fan mussel produces shiny gold-colored threads that attach it to the seabed. The threads are so fine that they attach themselves to individual grains of sand. The fiber is highly durable and doesn't fade; it was used in many areas along the shores of France, Britain, and the Mediterranean. Sea silk (not to be confused with fibers manufactured from a variety of marine materials and marketed under a similar trade name) is collected, carded, and spun; it's still produced in limited amounts in Italy. Pliny described the mussel as the "silkworm of the sea," but the fiber was also called "fish wool." Historians describe Henry II riding off to battle in a glorious tunic of golden sea silk; it was so striking that the battlefield is still called the Field of Gold.

Protein fibers are just a small part of the textile realm, but the incredible variety of fibers is a huge delight for the handspinner. From animals as large as bison and as small as spiders, protein fibers are a natural wonder and a testament to both nature's abundance and human ingenuity.

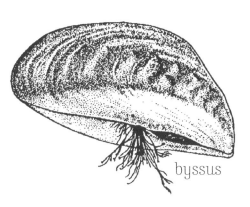

byssus

manufactured

Manufactured textile fibers are derived from either natural or chemical components. There are two types: regenerated fibers from natural sources such as bamboo, soy, milk products, or crustacean shells, and synthetic fibers made from any number of sources and created in a lab—test-tube fibers.

Why manufacture fiber when sheep and silk-worms do it naturally? The price and quality of wool and silk go up and down from year to year (as for all agricultural products), and they're seasonal and regional commodities. Imitations can be cheaper and more reliably produced than wool and silk. But scientists also developed artificial fibers because they could. Technology is often driven by a need to understand nature and to be free from a dependence on things beyond human control.

History of Fiber Biomimicry

In my textile collection, I have a pretty little white dress. It looks as if it walked out of a *Masterpiece Theatre* production, the perfect little dress for strawberry teas on the lawn of the manor house. It was collected in 1902 from a log cabin on the banks of the Missouri River in Montana, along with a boiled-wool Confederate uniform jacket. The top of the dress is silk, likely recycled from another garment; the skirt of the dress is a heavily patterned damask made from rayon.

When I was first offered this dress, I thought that the dates were wrong. Surely rayon was a fairly new fabric, a product of the surge of synthetics made in the United States after World War II. I was amazed to find that not only has rayon been produced since the 1880s, but also its origins and much of its manufacturing to this day are European.

During the 1800s, there was a huge explosion of manufactured fibers made from natural sources—cellulose, chitin-based fibers (from the shells of crabs, prawns, and shrimp), vegetable proteins such as soy, and animal proteins from milk products. The rise of scientific methods led to a greater understanding of natural processes. Scientists, having discovered how and what sheep and silkworms do, used biomimicry to imitate their processes and produce a wide range of fibers. Sheep and silkworms take cellulose in many forms—grass, weeds, shrubs, leaves—and turn them into protein, using water and sunlight. Their bodies are the "test tube" and the factory.

The rayon process was developed by a scientist who was working with silkworms.

Regenerated and synthetic fibers were developed to re-create the traits of natural fibers. This bamboo scarf, woven by Laura Fry, is smooth and shiny with a wonderful hand, qualities associated with silk.

To make silk, worms eat cellulose, digest it, turn it into a liquid protein, and spin it through little spinnerets, after which it is hardened with another protein spray. To make rayon, cellulose is ground, digested to form a liquid, and spun through little spinnerets, and another chemical is sprayed on them that hardens them into filaments.

Regenerated Cellulose

Cellulose is cellulose is cellulose: it doesn't matter what plant material it's obtained from. Fibers such as ramie, flax, and cotton have different appearances because their individual physical structure has been left intact. When plant materials have been digested (part of the pulp mill is called a digester), the result is pure cellulose. Whether called bamboo, Tencel, or viscose, it is all rayon, with rayon's benefits and drawbacks.

rayon

NANCY NEHRING

MAKING REGENERATED CELLULOSES

Two main methods produce regenerated cellulose, one more mainstream and one more eco-friendly; both require pulp mills.

Rayon was first developed in France in 1884 by Count Hilaire de Chardonnet, a student of Louis Pasteur. At that time, the silkworm industry was threatened by foul brood, a deadly strain of bacteria. Working with Pasteur to find a cure for this disease, de Chardonnet studied the process silkworms use to produce silk and was convinced he could make silk by some chemical means. Dissolving cellulose in alcohol and ether, he was able to produce an artificial fiber resembling silk. He was always careful to point out that he had not made silk, which is an animal product, but an artificial silk that was a vegetable product. The process de Chardonnet developed was the nitrocellulose process, and it produced an extremely flammable and explosive fiber.

After several ghastly accidents, the nitrocellulose process was replaced with the viscose process developed by three English chemists. Viscose was sold as artificial silk for many years. In 1924, the name rayon—chosen because the shiny surface of the fiber was like a ray of reflected sunlight—was taken as the generic name of all fibers made with regenerated cellulose. Today, rayon is the correct and legal name for all fibers made chemically from cellulose, regardless of the process used or the source of the fiber.

Viscose Process

The source of the cellulose—for example, eucalyptus (leaves, stems, and chipped trees), rapid growth poplar (leaves, stems, and chipped trees), bamboo (leaves, fine stems, and soft inner pulp from the trunk)—is crushed. This crushed material is soaked in a sodium-hydroxide solution, then heated to 77° Fahrenheit (25° Celsius) for several hours. The solution it forms is alkali cellulose. This mass is then strained and pressed to remove any excess sodium hydroxide, recrushed, and placed on screens to dry.

One part carbon disulfide is added to three parts alkali cellulose, which sulphurizes the cellulose and turns it into a jelly that rests for a while. After all the excess carbon disulphide evaporates, what remains is a new compound called cellulose sodium xanthogenate.

Sodium hydroxide is added to the cellulose sodium xanthogenate, which dissolves it and creates a viscose solution, about 5 percent sodium hydroxide and 15 percent cellulose. This viscose solution is forced through a spinneret (which functions like a silkworm's but looks like a shower head) into a vat of diluted sulfuric acid. The acid hardens the viscose cellulose xanthogenate, converting it into cellulose fibers that can be spun by traditional methods into yarn. Depending on the shape of the spinneret orifice, the fibers can be round, flat or U-shaped.

tencel

Lyocell

The more eco-friendly version is the chemical manufacturing process used to make lyocell from wood cellulose. This process, essentially the same as viscose, substitutes N-methylmorpholine-N-oxide for sodium hydroxide. N-methylmorpholine-N-oxide is thought to have fewer environmental issues than sodium hydroxide. The hardening bath for the lyocell process is a solution of water and some type of alcohol, usually methanol or ethanol.

Lyocell contains no free chlorine and is made in state-of-the-art low-emission pulp mills that recycle both the chemicals and the water used in the process. (More than 99 percent of all wastes, including waste water and air pollutants, is filtered and re-used.) Whenever possible, lyocell is made from farmed, sustainably grown trees. In 2000, the European Union gave this process an environmental award for sustainable development. This fiber process produces material with a wonderful drape that's naturally wrinkle-resistant (unlike many other rayons). The best known brand of lyocell is Tencel. SeaCell, a lyocell fiber that includes seaweed, has recently become available for handspinners.

The lyocell process has two drawbacks. Although it uses fewer environmentally damaging chemicals to produce the fiber, the process makes the fiber harder to dye than other types of rayon. To dye the fiber and make a cloth that won't fibrillate (or pill) requires additional chemical treatments.

Bamboo

Bamboo is a grass (not a tree) that can grow as much as 3 feet (.91 meters) in a day. Bamboo plants have natural defenses against insects and diseases; they grow easily without pesticides. Bamboo doesn't need massive cultivation; like other grasses, it grows up from a network of roots after it's cut. Like the grasses that sheep eat, it's a remarkably renewable resource. Because of its massive growth, bamboo consumes an enormous quantity of carbon from greenhouse gases, just like its slower cousins, the rangeland grasses.

Most bamboo fiber used to produce yarn comes from the leaves and the woody pith in the core of the plant, by-products of other uses including flooring, furniture, and building materials. In its natural fiber state, bamboo has a particularly high antibacterial, antifungal rating. The plant's natural fiber structure is full of microscopic air pockets, letting the fabric evaporate and absorb moisture.

Bamboo is processed in two ways to release the fiber: the viscose method (see page 48), which produces the vast majority of bamboo available for spinning, and the traditional method. The traditional method involves retting with bacteria and enzymes just as flax is processed (see page 16). The fibers are hackled, combed, and spun also like flax, and the material produced by this process is spun and woven and called bamboo linen. Until recently, the process was limited to artisan work and was extremely rare and expensive. Recently, it has been

bamboo

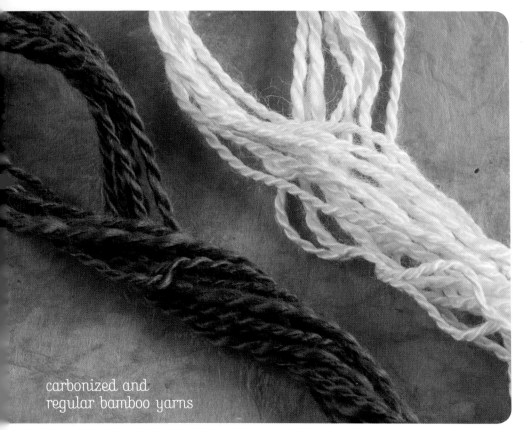

carbonized and
regular bamboo yarns

produced commercially in limited quantities for weavers and knitters. The fibers are short; bamboo is a jointed grass and doesn't have the length of a flax fiber. Unbleached, the fibers have the appearance and hand of hemp. They are not lustrous or silky.

All bamboo, traditional or extruded, is produced in countries other than the United States. The production of the fiber is regulated by the processing country's environmental regulations.

An interesting variation on extruded bamboo is carbonized bamboo. It is produced by a process called pyrolysis, which was developed by Thomas Edison in 1879 to make the filaments in electric lightbulbs. Carbonized bamboo is incredibly lightweight and strong; it has been used to make

airplanes, cars, and space equipment. The carbonized bamboo fiber spinners use has carbonized bamboo pulverized into a very fine powder impregnated into the bamboo fiber. The resulting fiber has excellent antifungal qualities and removes odors.

Azlon Fibers

Azlon is the name of the group of fibers made from regenerated proteins. Most of the fibers in this group came into commercial production in the 1930s and were produced until the 1960s, when low petroleum costs made synthetics much less expensive to produce. With today's increase in oil prices and growing environmental concerns, azlon fibers are being re-introduced. Formed by a process similar to the one that produces rayon, azlon fibers have been made with peanut protein (Ardil), corn (Zein), milk casein (Azlac), soybean, and chitin (coverings of crab, prawns, shrimp, and beetles). The protein is extracted, then dissolved into a solution. The solution is coagulated with the addition of another chemical, spun through a spinneret, hardened in a chemical bath, after which the fibers are collected and spun.

SOY

Soy fiber was developed in 1937—it was the fiber Henry Ford chose for his car upholstery. Like other azlon fibers, soy couldn't then compete with petroleum-based synthetics, but in 1997, the process was redeveloped in China. The new process adds chemical agents that make the fiber stronger and more breathable. Soy fiber is produced primarily from soy oil, a byproduct pressed from the soy cake that the soy food industry produces. The oil is cooked into a gel then treated to produce fibers. Soy fibers undergo a treatment called acetylating that involves the use of acetic acid, sulphuric acid, and hydrochloric acid. The fibers also require an additive to make them spinnable.

The natural color of soybean fiber is similar to a deep gold tussah silk, but it's usually bleached to remove the color and chemically scoured to remove any oil residues. Both processes make it easier to dye. Soybean fiber has wonderful luster and a soft, smooth hand. It doesn't take dye as well as silk, however, and is difficult to dye in deep shades.

Soy fiber has some natural antibacterial properties, but most are added to the fiber during the spinning process. Unlike polyester and acrylic textiles, the fiber is also biodegradable.

CASEIN

Casein fiber is produced from powdered skim, evaporated, or condensed milk. It takes 100 pounds (45.4 kilograms) of milk to produce 3 pounds (1.4 kilograms) of fiber in a process similar to that for soy fiber. Casein fibers are white, fluffy, and springy. Casein can't be distinguished from wool fiber by burning or chemical tests; you must use a microscope. Casein fiber has many of the properties of wool but is

soy silk

Corn fibers, corn-fiber yarn, corn kernels, and pellets from a stage of the production.

prices of synthetics rise. Regenerated corn fibers, called polylactics, are often blended with cotton and rayon. The result is soft and lustrous, with many of wool's best qualities; it is also wrinkle-resistant. However, it is difficult to dye at home and very heat-sensitive. The most common trade name for spinnable corn fiber is Ingeo.

CHITIN

Chitin is the major component in the exoskeletons of shrimp, crabs, prawns, and beetles. It's also present in the wings of grasshoppers and butterflies and in mushrooms and other fungi. Developed in the mid 1800s, chitin fiber's unique structure is neither cellulose nor protein, but between the two. It can be dyed with either cellulose or protein dyes. Originally used as medical cloth because of its amazing wound-healing abilities, chitin has become a popular addition to rayon, cotton, and wool yarns, especially those used for socks.

Chitin can be processed into sheets or fiber; it can also be ground into a powder in a process similar to that for making carbonized bamboo and similarly impregnated into another yarn. Scientists at Tottori University in Japan are exploring another interesting application: using chitin to bond fragrance to silk yarns.

Synthetic Fibers

Synthetic fibers are made wholly from chemicals, mostly petrochemicals, and form new components that don't exist in nature.

weaker and generally used in wool blends. Casein doesn't attract moths, and its very even micron count gives it a smooth and silky hand with no prickle factor. When it is wet, however, casein tends to smell like sour milk. It is also extremely fragile when wet and mildews easily.

CORN

Corn contains abundant protein; more than 30 percent of its composition is a protein called *zein*. From the 1930s until the 1960s, this protein was processed to produce fiber. It dyed and washed easily but was mostly used in blends because it was weak and shrank significantly. Like soybean and casein fiber, it's enjoying a comeback as the

Acrylic, polyester, and nylon are all synthetics made from petroleum, but thousands of synthetic fibers are in production. Although most aren't spun by handspinners, some, such as nylon and metallized fiber, are occasionally used in fiber blends or as a binder.

NYLON

Nylon is the most common synthetic handspinners use, either by itself or in combination with wool. It is an isomer (a left-hand equation, or molecule with nearly identical structure and the same atomic makeup) of wool and imitates wool fairly well. It takes wool dyes (naturally derived and synthetic) well—often better than wool does. It is frequently used to increase wool's strength, as an addition to sock yarns or a supporting thread in novelty yarns. It is also used to increase a yarn's spinnability by decreasing the average micron (see page 58) and to decrease the cost of yarn.

Nylon is formed by a process called polymerization, whereby small molecules join to form large molecules. DuPont Company scientists found that certain chemicals would combine to form superpolymers, which could be drawn out or extruded into filaments. The first nylon, produced in 1939, was made with coal, air, and water: hydrocarbon from coal, nitrogen and oxygen from air, and hydrogen from water. The list of ingredients has expanded to include natural gas and petroleum combined with chemicals made from agricultural waste such as corncobs, cottonseed hulls, rice hulls, and oat hulls.

metallized fibers

METALLIZED FIBERS

Lurex, Angelina, and Firestar are the best-known trade names for fibers that have had metal fused to them. Made by vaporizing colored aluminum onto a film of rayon, nylon, or polyester and cutting it to the appropriate width, these fibers have become increasingly complex. They're now available not only in light-reflective but also in light-refractive and holographic forms.

manufactured

science of fibers

One of the many things I have learned as a working craftsperson is that good design is not simply a matter of good taste—it requires good science as well. I have worked during a period of massive diversion and division; in my lifetime, science and art have split apart, and the ever-widening gap has become an intellectual continental drift.

But working with primary materials and transforming them into objects requires a deep understanding of material. Good science preserves and supports good design; developing an understanding of fibers, their possibilities and their limitations, has an enormous impact on the work of a fiber artist.

Fiber Characteristics

How will fibers work for you? What can you expect from them? How will they react in a mixture? What will add loft, what will add luster? Every fiber artist asks these (and a few thousand more) questions. For spinners, it's doubly important because the character of the cloth is made on the spinning wheel. No matter how you construct the cloth, the characteristics of the fiber, spinning, and finishing let fabric do some things and not others. Wishing won't make a silky fiber such as bamboo smooth, lustrous, and long-wearing; spinning a firm worsted will.

Identifying Fibers

Fiber artists are true descendants of hunter-gatherer societies, especially the gathering part! Using mill waste, finding odd lots of fiber on the Internet, and checking bargain sales are all part of our craft. Sometimes fibers and yarns aren't identified or are labeled incorrectly. To help sort out what is in the stash, here are a few simple tests.

BLEACH TEST

Conduct this test carefully in a well-ventilated area. Weigh the sample material, then add it to pure household bleach in a stainless steel pan. Bring the bleach to a boil and stir with a wooden dowel or wooden spoon for ten minutes. Let cool; skim off the fibers and let them dry. Weigh the sample again. If it's lighter, then the bleach dissolved keratin-based fibers such as wool. What remains by weight is the part of the sample that isn't keratin-based fiber. Fiber-Etch, a product used by fiber artists to create dévoré fabric by dissolving cellulose fibers, can be used to find the cellulose fiber composition.

 cellulose

Characteristics of Bast Fiber

- Coarse-pored; absorbs and releases moisture rapidly
- Strongest type of vegetable fiber
- Stronger when wet than dry
- Excellent tensile strength
- Not damaged by soaps or detergents
- Resistant to damage by sunlight
- Antibacterial, antimicrobial, and antifungal properties
- Lack of lint
- Smooth surface
- Difficult to dye
- Resists stains

Characteristics of Cotton and Other Seed-Hair Fiber

- Finest of natural fibers
- Very uniform micron; exceptionally soft hand
- Coarse-pored; absorbs and releases moisture rapidly
- Tolerates solvents (easily dry cleaned)
- Not damaged by soaps or detergents
- Resistant to damage by bleach
- Machine washable and dryable
- Damaged by long exposure to sunlight
- Damaged by mildew and rot-producing bacteria
- Damaged by silverfish
- Can be sewn easily
- Can be ironed easily
- Low luster unless treated by mercerization
- Good color retention when dyed

 protein

Characteristics of Keratin-Based Fiber

- Thermodynamic (hot in cold weather, cool in hot weather)
- Generates heat when wet
- Holds moisture without feeling wet
- Generally weaker when wet; strength returns when dry
- Most elastic natural fiber
- Good resistance to abrasion
- Medium tensile strength
- Pliable
- Felts (unique among textile fibers)
- Sensitive to alkalis (especially when used with heat)
- Weakened by chlorine bleach
- Damaged by moths and carpet beetles
- Damaged by molds, bacteria, and mildew
- Dyes easily
- Holds stains and traps dirt

Characteristics of Fibroin-Based Fiber

- Great natural length
- Finest natural fiber
- Strongest natural fiber
- Weaker when wet; strength returns when dry
- Resilient
- Turns yellow with high heat
- Damaged by alkalis
- Not affected by weak acids
- Damaged slightly by sunlight
- Poor conductor of heat
- Poor conductor of electricity
- Dyes easily
- Sheds dirt
- Absorbs oils
- High luster

manufactured

Characteristics of Manufactured Fiber

- Can be made in any length needed
- Can be made to any crimp needed
- Can be extruded to any diameter or shape needed
- Stronger than most natural fibers
- Often weaker when wet; strength returns when dry

- Generally poor elasticity
- Poor resistance to sun damage
- Can be dyed in spinning solution
- Many have antibacterial, antimicrobial properties
- Good resistance to damage by chlorine bleach
- Low resistance to high heat

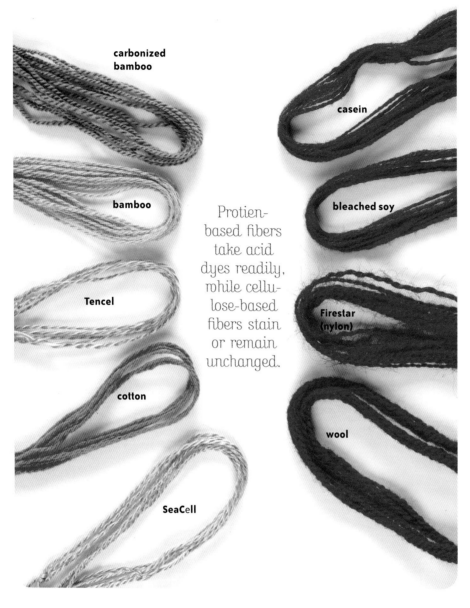

carbonized bamboo

casein

bamboo

bleached soy

Tencel

Protien-based fibers take acid dyes readily, while cellulose-based fibers stain or remain unchanged.

Firestar (nylon)

cotton

wool

SeaCell

the flame and watch: Does the fiber move? Which way? Move the fiber into the flame. Watch how it catches fire and what the flame looks like. Take it out of the flame and watch: Does it continue to burn? Does it immediately go out? Does it smoke? Smell the burned fiber. Examine the ash. Keep notes. Be cautious; fibers such as flax, bamboo, and acrylic burn instantly and very hot. Fibers that burn when directly exposed to flame but go out when the flame is removed are called "self-extinguishing."

WEAK ACID DYE TEST

Use any dye that works on wool with a simple acid such as vinegar. (If you don't usually use dyes, Kool-aid will work.) Put a small sample in a stainless steel pot, cover it with water, and add 1 tablespoon vinegar and enough dye to color the water. Bring to a boil, remove from the heat, and let cool. Rinse the sample. If it's a protein-based fiber (like wool, silk, angora, cashmere, or soya), it should easily rinse clear, leaving the fiber dyed. Protein fibers, including vegetable-based ones, will accept acid dyes. (Any dye that is heat-set will be difficult to use with corn fiber.) Because nylon is an imitation of keratin, it can also be dyed with acid dyes; it actually takes many dyes better than wool. Cellulose fibers (cotton, flax, ramie, hemp), reconstructed cellulosic fibers (rayon, Tencel, bamboo), and acrylic and polyester won't accept this dye.

Fiber by the Numbers: Fineness and Consistency

Most of the measurements and tests introduced below gauge the fineness and consistency of fibers. Fineness matters for two reasons: it defines the "spinning limit" (or spinning potential) and influences the

FIBER ROTATION TEST

You will need a microscope for this test; an inexpensive handheld one with 100× magnification will be strong enough. Soak a small amount of fiber in water. Take a few fibers and warm them with a lamp. With the microscope, watch to see whether they move. Cellulose fibers rotate; protein fibers do not. Flax and ramie rotate to the left, cotton and hemp to the right.

BURN TEST

Burn tests are helpful to identify fibers; they also show you how the finished fabric will react if it catches fire. Burn tests are quite simple, but do take a few precautions before you start. I use a candle and place the candlestick in a pan of water to minimize fire risk. Start by burning a few fibers whose content you know so you can compare the results. Move the fiber near

Burn Test Results

Cellulose

	FLAME TYPE	HOW DOES IT BURN?	BURNING SMELL	SMOKE	ASH
COTTON	Orange-yellow; unbleached cotton has a slight violet shade at base of flame.	Ignites quickly. Burns steadily. Not self-extinguishing. Can be blown out. Does not fuse or move away from flame.	Burned paper.	Smokes after flames are extinguished; bluish smoke.	Leaves a black ash skeleton; soft, not greasy or crisp.
FLAX	Orange and yellow; some sparking.	Ignites easily and rapidly, producing a large flame. Not self-extinguishing. Can be blown out. Fiber is crisp near the flame. Does not fuse, melt, or move away from flame.	Grass fire.	Smokes after flames are extinguished; bluish smoke.	Fragile gray ash skeleton.
HEMP	Yellow in the middle, top, and bottom. Changes to orange.	Ignites easily and rapidly. Not self-extinguishing. No melting.	Burned paper.	Smokes after flame is extinguished; bluish wisps.	Fragile white ash skeleton.
RAMIE	Yellow at center of flame, orange around edges and top and bottom.	Ignites quickly. Burns very fast. Not self-extinguishing. No melting.	Burned paper.	Smokes after flame is extinguished; wisps of blue smoke.	Fragile black ash.

Protein

	FLAME TYPE	HOW DOES IT BURN?	BURNING SMELL	SMOKE	ASH
SILK	Orange-yellow with an orange top; some sparking.	Ignites easily. Burns unsteadily with a slight crackle. Self-extinguishing. Can't be easily blown out.	Burned hair or burned eggs.	Bluish gray after it's removed from the flame.	Very black, crisp; holds its shape.
WOOL	Yellow with orange top and purple to blue bottom.	Ignites readily but rapidly self-extinguishes (hard to keep ignited). Burns slowly. Fuses and curls away from the flame. Swells when burning. Long wools crackle.	Burned hair.	Bluish-gray clouds when removed from the flame.	Crisp, black, puffy ash.
ALPACA	Yellow and gold.	Hard to ignite; won't easily hold a flame. Burns slowly. Fiber bubbles and swells when burning.	Very strong smell of burned hair.	Smoldering smoke; grayish blue and wispy.	Crisp, shiny ash that holds its shape.

Manufactured

	FLAME TYPE	HOW DOES IT BURN?	BURNING SMELL	SMOKE	ASH
NYLON	Orange edges, blue body with orange tip; hisses.	Melts. Doesn't ignite readily. Will burn rapidly after it melts if kept in the flame. Self-extinguishing. Yarn moves away from the flame.	Acrid; a bit like celery.	Gray-blue puffs.	Leaves no ash; melts and leaves a hard black irregular bead.
RAYON	Yellow edges with orange center; some sparks.	Ignites very easily. Burns rapidly. Not self-extinguishing. Does not shrink away from the flame.	Burning leaves.	Bluish smoke when flame is extinguished.	Black or gray ash.
ACRYLIC	Yellow.	Ignites instantly. Burns hot. Splatters and melts; melted drops continue to burn. Difficult to extinguish.	Acrid and harsh.	Acrid, black.	Hard black tar residue.

"comfort factor" rating (see below). The more fibers a yarn has, the more uniform the yarn will be; it will also be stronger and softer to the touch.

SPINNING COUNT

The spinning count is a system developed to classify wool and give the expected yardage that could be spun from it. The count system is still widely used both in industry and by craftspeople. Developed in Britian, it is often referred to as the Bradford count. The spinning count of a fiber equals the number of standard-sized hanks that can be spun from a pound of fleece; it's given for worsted and woolen spinning.

This system measures two things: the fineness of the fleece and the yardage in a given yarn. For example, using the worsted spinning count, a pound of 60s fleece is capable of producing sixty 560-yard (512-meter) hanks of singles, while a pound of 54s fleece would produce fifty-four hanks. (The "s" indicates that the yarn is singles.) Under the woolen system, the same pound of 60s fleece would produce sixty 1,600-yard (1463-meter) skeins. Using this system to measure fleeces, the finer the fleece, the bigger the number.

The Bradford count is also used to describe yarns: a yarn that's labeled 60/2 means that the singles (60) have either 60 × 560 yards (512 meters) or 60 × 1,600 yards (1,463 meters) per pound. The 2 indicates it's two-ply. To find the yards per pound for this yarn, multiply the 60 by 560 (yards per skein for worsted) and divide by two. For woolen, multiply the 60 by 1,600 (yards per skein of woolen) and divide by two.

How can you tell if the yarn is worsted or woolen spun? The numbers used to be reversed: worsted was described as 2/60 and a woolen was 60/2. It's unusual for the order of the numbers to describe the different types of spinning today, but it's still useful to know. No matter the order of the numbers, one gives the number of plies, and, just as for fleece, the bigger the other number, the finer the yarn.

MICRON

A micron is a metric unit of measurement equal to one-millionth of a meter. Micron count is used to describe the average micron of a particular fiber. For instance, vicuña has an average micron count of 10, alpaca has a micron count of 18, and llama has a micron count of 24. Higher numbers indicate coarser fibers.

To determine the micron count of a fiber, samples are examined with either a Laserscan or an Optical Fiber Diameter Analyser (OFDA), which measure accurately to within a micron. A Laserscan micron report gives both the average fiber diameter in microns and the standard deviation, or the percentage of fibers that are smaller or larger than the average diameter. Recent fiber studies have shown a definite relationship between the prickliness of a fiber (now called the prickle factor) and the standard deviation. There is also a relationship between fineness and deviation; most fibers with a micron count less than 21.5 show little to no variation in micron. The OFDA can also measure the degree of medullation (see page 26) present in a fiber sample; when the medulla is greater than 60 percent, the fibers are classed as kemp, an undesirable characteristic.

Most micron tests also include a report on the percentage of fibers with a micron

mcmorran balance

count of more than 30, which is used to determine the fiber's comfort factor. The percentage of fibers with a micron count of more than 30 subtracted from 100 percent. For example, if 6 percent of the fibers in a sample are more than 30 microns, the comfort factor would be 94 percent. There is also a mathematical relationship between the number of crimps in a fiber and the fiber's fineness: the higher the number of crimps, the finer the fiber.

DENIER

A denier is a unit of measurement based on the weight of a Roman coin. It was the standard unit of measurement for reeled silk; it is also currently used to measure all extruded fibers such as rayon and nylon. The standard is based on one pound of 1 denier filament, measuring 4,464,528 yards. To find the yardage of any yarn listed by denier, divide the number into 4,464,528 yards. For example, a 15-denier filament would have 297,635.2 yards per pound. Using the denier system, the smaller the number, the finer the filament.

Tensile and Abrasion Strength

The two main strengths for which fibers are tested are tensile strength and resistance to withstand abrasion. Tensile strength means how much resistance a fiber has to a force tending to pull it apart. Tests show that wool is stronger than cotton but weaker than silk, and all three are weaker than nylon. However, wool and silk have a far greater tensile strength than steel, because wool and silk are elastic while steel is not.

Abrasion is wear caused by rubbing; the wear on the heel of a sock is a classic example of wear from abrasion. Abrasion is tested by seeing how long it takes to break through a fiber by rubbing. The longer and finer a fiber is, the better it can naturally withstand the forces of abrasion.

Tools for Measuring Yarn and Fiber

Although many of the measurements described above can only be tested in a specialized laboratory, a few simple relatively low-tech devices can tell you a lot about your fiber and yarn. Two of them are a McMorran Balance and a handheld microscope.

McMORRAN BALANCE

The McMorran balance is a deceptively simple and incredibly useful tool! It measures the yards per pound in any yarn. If you're trying to duplicate a yarn, either handspun or commercial, the first thing

you need to know is the number of yards per pound (ypp) of the yarn. When you're spinning yarn for use with a commercial pattern, knowing the ypp of the suggested commercial yarn is crucial to making a successful substitution.

McMorran balances are easy to use: Place the box on a flat surface and put the balance arm in the notched area at the top of the box. Cut a piece of yarn (err on the side of a too-long piece) and hang it over the balance arm, which will drop like a weighted seesaw. It may be necessary to move the balance so the yarn can hang over the edge of the table. Patiently snip off bits of yarn in small increments until the arm balances. Measure the remaining yarn in inches. Try not to stretch it, but hold it even and straight. Multiply the number of inches by 100 to find the number of yards per pound. Nothing tricky, no need for a calculator—if the yarn measures 11¾ inches (29.8 centimeters), then there are 1,175 yards (1,074.4 meters) per pound.

To measure a textured or variegated-thickness yarn, measure three lengths and take the average to find the most accurate yardage. Especially in a dry climate, the plastic box can become highly charged, and static glues the yarn to the box. Use an antistatic cloth or a dryer sheet to discharge it. Occasionally, I've met people who have never been able to get an accurate reading with their balances; I discovered that the balances they were using worked perfectly, but in metric measurements. Their balances had been mislabeled.

HANDHELD MICROSCOPE

This is a useful tool no matter what area of textiles interests you. An inexpensive handheld microscope is handy for examining textiles, yarn structures, and fiber structure. Microscopes commonly come in 7, 30, and 100 times magnification. The 7× is quite accurate for examining textile structures; the 100× is great for examining fibers. You can see the variation in size between the fibers and identify kemp fibers; you can even see the surface of many fibers quite well. Scientific tool suppliers and stores for naturalists often carry handheld microscopes.

handheld microscope

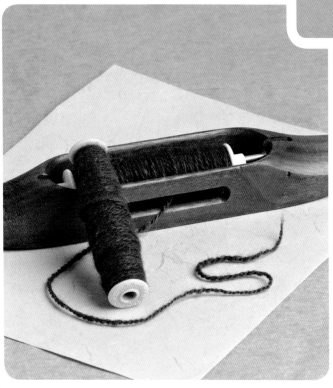

spinning techniques

WHEN I LEARNED TO SPIN, my teacher spun beautifully—and had strong opinions about spinning that had served her well. She had earned the right to those opinions. For her, there were two types of spinning: worsted and wrong.

Imagine my surprise when, years later and far from our village, I tried to spin cotton and found that nothing in my spinning experience helped. Cashmere wasn't easy either, and my spun angora was like wire. I experimented and struggled for several months until I found a method that worked and made spinning those short crimpy fibers a joy and a pleasure. When I finally met other spinners, I discovered that the technique I had re-invented was woolen spinning.

There is no right or wrong way to spin, but like everything else, spinning is governed by cause and effect: if you do this, that will happen. When you understand the forces at work in your yarn, you can choose (and even modify) any of the basic spinning methods to get exactly the yarn you want from the fiber you choose.

CHAPTER FIVE

drafting methods

DRAFTING TECHNIQUES make fiber do specific things—think of them as tools to make beautiful yarns. They are related, like a big sprawling family full of brothers and sisters. How do they differ? It all has to do with the way the twist goes in.

Worsted yarns are created when twist enters fibers that are already attenuated, or stretched out and held under tension. The fibers are drawn up into the drafting zone parallel to one another as the spinner drafts forward, keeping twist out of the fibers being drafted, and then allows the twist to enter while the fibers are still under tension. Because they are held under pressure, fibers stay in order, not moving sideways or buckling.

Woolen yarns are made when twist is released into the loose fibers. Like a whirlpool, the twist swirls and tangles the fibers together. These tangled fibers are then stretched out away from the wheel as more twist is added to spin them into yarn. Unlike worsted spinning, twist enters the fibers before and during attenuation.

Semiworsted and *semiwoolen* describe methods that combine some traits of both worsted and woolen methods (including fiber choice, preparation, and drafting).

Whether a yarn falls more on the side of woolen or worsted depends on how the twist is entered into the fibers: twist before drafting is semiwoolen; twist after drafting is semiworsted.

Slub and *bouclé* drafts march to the beat of their own drummer. Spinners use both to change the surface texture of yarn while maintaining its structural integrity.

The Worsted Family

Worsted comes first, not because it's better or more important than other methods but because it's how humans first started spinning. It's the simplest form of spinning and takes the least amount of coordination. All other methods build on the skills and muscle acquired by learning to spin worsted.

Worsted-spun yarns have distinct characteristics. Because of their smooth, even surfaces, they easily shed water, snow, and dirt, making them the perfect choice for upholstery and carpet yarns. They resist pilling and felting, making hard-wearing smooth-surfaced knitted or woven fabrics. For knitting, worsted-spun yarns have the best stitch definition and are used when the clear visibility of the stitch is a major design element. Sock yarns are generally

wheel mechanics

SPINNING WHEELS are combinations of several simple mechanisms, mostly the lever, wheel, and pulley. Although spinners often use their own terminology to discuss wheels, understanding the scientific principles behind them can help you use the wheel to your advantage.

When you turn the drive wheel, the drive band turns one or more pulleys. Spinners usually call these pulleys "whorls," but that term refers to a component of a handspindle, which serves a different function. (The size of the pulley on a spinning wheel actually works more like the shaft diameter of a spindle.)

In single-drive systems, such as those with scotch or irish tension, the drive wheel turns only one pulley, either on the bobbin or the flyer. The brake or tension is applied to the other and is used to adjust the drafting-in speed. This is the most common way of adjusting the draw-in or take-up of the yarn being spun. In double-drive systems, one drive band turns the pulley on both the flyer and the bobbin. The closer in diameter these pulleys are, the less drafting-in speed.

On both systems, increasing the tension on the drive band increases the drafting-in speed.

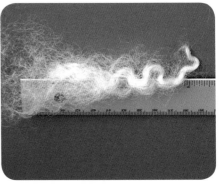

More than 2½" long and with fewer than seven crimps per inch, this wool is a good choice for worsted spinning.

spun worsted for durability and for the comfort the evenly entered twist gives to the foot. Overshot and tapestry weaving use worsted yarns for the same reason, while satin weaves make use of their smooth, highly reflective surfaces. Stitch definition and the ability to withstand abrasion make worsted the perfect choice for embroidery yarns and sewing yarns.

Worsted yarns do have drawbacks. Worsted-spun yarn is heavier than woolen-spun yarn because the ideal fibers, stretched flat during drafting and selected to have less crimp, are packed more densely together. A good worsted yarn contains 75 to 80 percent air, while a good woolen is 90 to 97 percent air. Because there is less trapped air to provide thermal mass, worsted yarns don't have the warmth of woolen yarns. Traditionally made with low-crimp fibers, true worsted yarns don't have as much memory as woolen yarns do. Good worsted yarn requires the best quality fiber; only the cream of the world's wool supply is high enough quality to be combed for worsted spinning.

Although any variation on twist entering attenuated fibers creates a worsted-style yarn, a true worsted yarn has three main ingredients: the right fiber, the right preparation, and the right draw.

FIBER

Choose fiber that has a staple longer than 2½ inches (6.5 centimeters) and fewer than seven crimps per inch. Flax, hemp, ramie, silk, alpaca, and llama are all perfect for spinning worsted. Most of the regenerated cellulose fibers, such as bamboo and Tencel (lyocell), are best spun worsted. Luster longwool sheep, including Romney, Border Leicester, Lincoln, Teeswater, and Cotswold, have been bred to produce fleece ideally suited for traditional worsted spinning.

Choosing Fleece

When you buy a fleece (of any fiber, not just wool) with the intention of spinning a perfect worsted yarn, check its strength. Take a staple (the naturally occurring division of the fiber, like a lock of hair) and give it three good strong snaps—not just pulls—between your hands. It shouldn't break. If it does, put the fleece back. If it passes, take another staple and hold it beside your ear. Give it the same firm snap and listen carefully for a crackling sound; snap it and listen twice more. A perfect fleece will not crackle but have a resonant twang like a guitar string. The clearer the sound, the stronger the fiber. The crackling sound, produced by some of the fibers breaking, means the fleece is "tender." If the crackling diminishes through the three snaps, it has a smaller percentage of breaks than if it crackles continuously. Tender fleeces can be combed to remove the weak fibers, but more fiber will be lost than from a strong fleece.

Pay careful attention to the crimp structure, making sure that the crimp falls within the guidelines for a good worsted fleece. You might want a crimpier fleece for several reasons—for a perfect sock yarn, for

instance, where elasticity is important—but for a classic worsted yarn, the fiber should have seven or fewer crimps per inch.

Vegetable matter isn't a concern for fibers that will be combed because combing removes most debris. However, it will affect the amount of usable spinning fiber per pound.

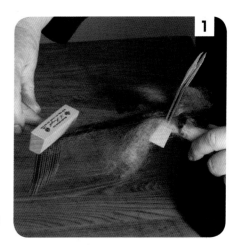

PREPARATION

You can prepare fibers for worsted spinning many ways, but all have the same goal: to align the fibers so that they're parallel and remove any fibers that are weak or short. Although plenty of tools are available for combing fiber, your tool needn't be expensive. My friend Fiona spun and knitted her first sweater when she was an exchange student on a Romney sheep station in New Zealand. In the evening, she and the station owners sat around the dinner table by lantern light and combed the lovely silky locks with their forks. A three-ply beauty, that sweater still looks good after thirty years of use. Other inexpensive tools for combing are dog brushes, flickers, and mini-combs.

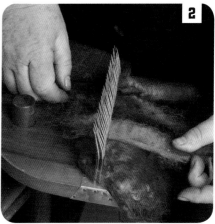

To make a traditional worsted yarn, you need proper wool combs; you'll find it impossible to produce true top with anything else. You can choose from a variety of combs, including simple handheld minicombs (choose the two-row style if you're buying a pair), **1** Russian paddle combs, **2** and Dutch or English wool combs. **3** All of these combs will separate the different lengths of fleece as well as catch the weak, broken, and short crimpy fibers behind the tines (teeth) on the combs.

Before you invest in a set of combs, find a way to try a variety of them. See what works

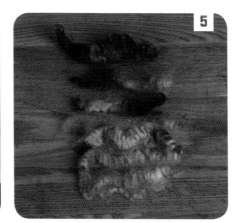

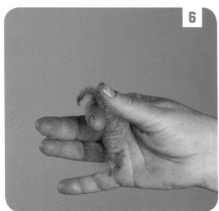

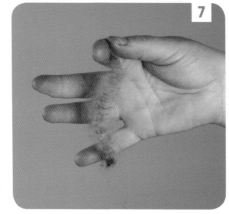

best for the type of fibers you're interested in—and see if the process is right for you at all. I recommend multipitch combs; "pitch" refers to the number of rows of tines. The tines are staggered so that the fiber can be combed finer. The longer the pitch is, the longer the fiber will have to be in order to fit on the combs. The finer the tines and the closer they are, the finer the fiber you can comb.

For very fine fibers, such as bombyx silk, fine angora, and vicuña, even the finest combs aren't fine enough. I use a pair of cotton cards as if they were combs and spin off the tip of the cards. **4** It's easy to spin a fine, perfect thread this way, and it's a great method for making your own blends as well.

Sort and Wash

Before you comb the fiber, sort it by staple length and wash it. One of the advantages of making your own top rather than buying it ready-made—the difference between homemade bread fresh from the oven and week-old Wonder Bread—is that you can keep the staples in order. In commercial top, the cut and tip ends are intermingled. True worsted is spun with the locks all going one way: from the tip.

Stapling—sorting fleece by lock length and crimp type—makes a huge difference to the fiber quality. **5** After you've sorted the locks by length and type, wash them as clean as possible while maintaining the lock structure. You can keep fleece in order while it's being washed several ways. Serious lace spinners wash it by hand, one lock at a time. I wash mine by fitting a cloth inside a rectangular stainless steel roasting pan, then heating it on the stovetop. (For a detailed explanation, see "On Washing Fleece," *Spin·Off* magazine, Fall 2008.)

Washing the fiber well before combing or carding helps separate the individual fibers. When they absorb water in the washing process, fibers swell and straighten, often becoming three times larger than when dry. They also become longer because the crimp is released in the washing process. Combing wool that was well-soaked during washing was a traditional method used by the woolcomber guilds in Britain, and one that I've used with both combing and carding. It also prevents the fibers from flying out of order because of static.

Comb

If fibers are dry, or you are combing and spinning in dry conditions, static can be a problem. To alleviate static, you may choose to add oil during combing, a traditional requirement for true worsted spinning. Fill a spray bottle with three parts water and one part oil—almost any light oil will do. Some spinners enjoy a light essential oil with a mild scent to it such as lavender.

Load the washed locks of fiber on the stationary comb with the cut ends close to the handle. (If you can't immediately tell which is the tip end, hold the washed lock loosely between your thumb and forefinger and gently rub your fingers back and forth ⬛6; the scales on the fiber will "walk" toward the tip end. ⬛7) This process is called "lashing on" or "charging." ⬛8 Fill the combs about two-thirds full. Spray the locks with the oil-water mixture until they're damp but not dripping. Spray again during the combing process whenever the locks become charged with static.

Heat helps to keep fibers relaxed during the combing process, and hot combs will pass through more easily, with the added benefit of evenly distributing moisture from the oil-water mixture used to minimize static. I use my combs hot enough to be uncomfortable to touch; I keep the tines in hot water from a little electric hot pot until I'm ready to comb. Pass the comb through the locks from top to bottom, starting with just the tips and working your way up until all the tangles are removed. ⬛9

Next, change the combing direction—swing the comb sideways through the fibers. ⬛10 Don't be gentle; you want to remove any weak fibers. The fiber will transfer from the stationary comb to the working comb. As it's transferred, the end of the locks secured in the teeth will change with each pass. When you start, the shorn end will be secured in the stationary combs; during your first combing pass, the fibers that transfer to the working comb will now

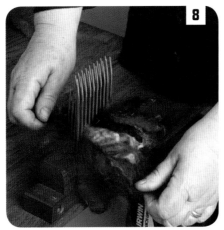

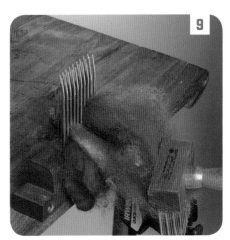

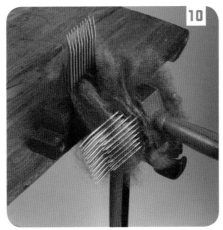

have the tip end in the comb and the shorn end loose. ⬛11 When you're combing fleece, be careful to keep track of whether the cut end or tip end is being combed.

Depending on the type of combs you use, exchange the position of the combs and start again or recharge the fiber onto the stationary comb. Do this as many times as is necessary to open up the fibers you're using. Stop on a pass where the cut end is combed, leaving the tip end at the front of the comb. Traditional combers would use three or four sets of combs, each one

finer than the last, to produce the best top possible. If you're fortunate to have more than one set of combs, remove the fibers from the first set of combs and lash it onto the next finest set of combs.

Use a diz to remove the fiber from the comb. (In some cases, you may want to skip the diz and simply spin from the combs.) Choose a diz with a hole similar to the diameter of yarn you want to spin; you can spin finer than the diz size but not larger. ⬛12 To start using the diz, take just the very tips of the fiber on your stationary

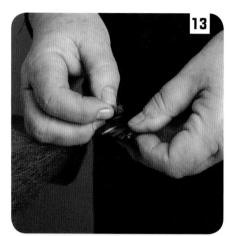

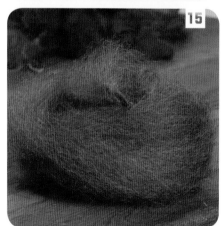

combs and twist it for an inch or two, then let the fibers fold back on themselves. **13**

Insert a threading hook through the hole in the diz and catch the loop of twisted fibers you just formed at the tip of your combed locks. Gently pull the loop through the hole in the diz and remove the threading hook. Slowly draft the fibers off the combs through the hole in the diz, **14** moving the diz back and forth across the combed fibers and drafting through it until you've removed everything but waste from the stationary comb. You will know when you come to the waste fiber: the fiber will not pull easily through the diz. (Save the waste from combing as long as it isn't too chaffy. It will be perfect for spinning woolen.) The twisted portion will tell you where to start spinning—it is the tip end. **15** Bast fibers are prepared similarly, by drawing the fibers through finer and finer combs until the waste is removed. **16** **17** Remember to keep the root and blossom ends in order and spin from the blossom end.

Choosing Prepared Fiber

If you're buying already prepared fiber to make a worsted yarn, choose top rather than a carded preparation. Carding is used primarily to mix fibers of different lengths and micron counts together. Carding deliberately crosses the fibers to produce a web, rather than aligning the fibers parallel as in combing. Not only are the fibers in top similar in length and micron, the combing process has removed weak, broken, and damaged fibers. Most top has also been hot pressed—a process similar to steam ironing—to deactivate crimp in the fiber, making it draft as smoothly as possible.

If you're not sure whether you have top or roving, grasp it firmly in two hands and pull until it separates. If the fibers separate cleanly, leaving a straight line, the fiber is top.  (Fibers that have been dyed as top, however, are less aligned because the water of the dye bath disarranges them and reactivates the crimp.) If it's ragged and uneven, the fiber is roving.

WORSTED DRAW

Sometimes called short draw, forward draw, or inch-worming, worsted is the slowest of the spinning draws. It produces the most perfectly even yarn and the most reflective of all spinning surfaces. When you spin worsted, everything is in order: all the fibers go in the same direction and the twist enters already attenuated fibers. All drafting is done toward the wheel. Aim for an even amount of twist and an even diameter. In worsted spinning, what you see is what you get. Take anything that isn't perfect—slubs, tight places, vegetable matter, stains—out while you're spinning the singles. (They'll be harder to remove later and may leave marks.)

To spin with a worsted draw, hold the combed top in your fiber-supply hand, with the tip end forward. If you've combed the top yourself, you'll know where the tip is. But commercial top is also directional. Spin in the direction it drafts out more easily. Join the top to the leader by placing the fiber between the two ends of the leader. 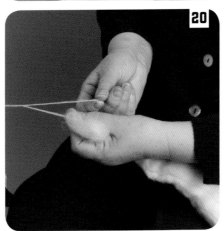 Use your drafting hand to gently pull fibers forward out of your supply, simultaneously keeping twist from entering these fibers as you draft them forward toward the wheel's orifice.  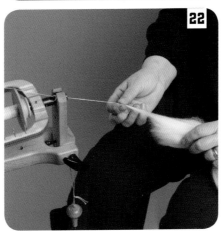 Once you have the fibers drafted, gently slide your drafting hand back, smoothing down the attenuated fibers and allowing the twist to follow your fingers down—but never allowing the twist past your fingers.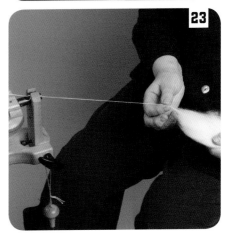

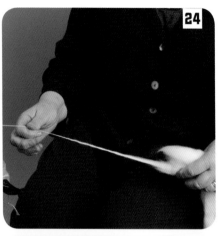

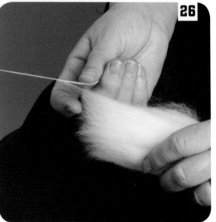

to, break the yarn, pull the fibers back into order as much as possible, and rejoin it. Use a good worsted join by letting some of the loose fiber feather into the end of the yarn. **26** Remember to draft toward the wheel. (Drafting away from the wheel will cause a slub at the join. **27** **28**)

Problems, Pitfalls, and Helpful Hints

● Try not to let the twist slip past your fingers. Twist is like glue; it holds fibers (and the textile world) together. If the twist slips by your fingers into the top, where all the fibers are aligned, it will simply glue it shut. No amount of pulling will draft the fibers forward.

● Don't open your fingers; use your most articulate hand—the one with the best motor skills—to control the twist. Adjusting the drafting-in speed so that it pulls the yarn onto the bobbin slightly faster will often solve the problem.

● Having trouble drafting commercial top? **29** Try spinning from the other end. Top has a definite grain caused by the direction of the industrial carding and combing teeth. To make sure that you're drafting from the right end of the fiber, just give it a tug, first one way, then the other. Draft in the direction that pulls out most easily. **30**

If spinning worsted is new to you, it may literally get out of hand. Left to its own devices, the twist would run through all the fibers in your hand. **24**

When twist runs into fibers that aren't stretched out, it moves the fiber in a circular motion, like a washing machine. This motion crosses the fibers, making them weaker and duller. When you get twist in the web (already drafted fibers), stop and let some of the twist run out of the fiber by untwisting it with your fingers and drafting out more fibers. **25** If you have

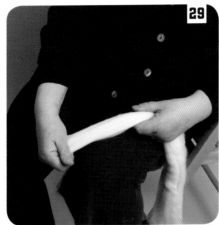
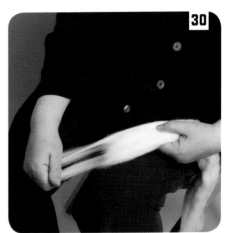

- Learn to go back and forth across the top of the web, not down the side.
- If you have continual problems with commercial top, try spinning the top with some of its crimp reactivated. Just soak the top in hot water, roll it in a towel, and spin the excess water out. When it's dry, it will be springy and much easier to draft—even if a little twist slips by. It will produce a slightly different yarn than true worsted.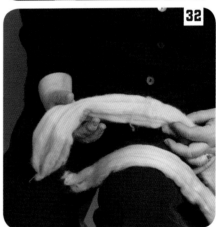

The Woolen Family

Woolen spinning gives yarn a soft matte finish that obscures the stitch, whether it's used for knitting or weaving. It produces the softest and lightest yarn because a good woolen yarn contains more than 90 percent air. Woolen-spun yarn has good memory and resilience. Shetland sweaters are a classic use for woolen-spun knitting yarn. With a distinctive surface that slightly softens complex knitted patterns, these sweaters are lightweight and warm. Cashmere is generally spun woolen for garments that are both warm and light, with a rich matte finish that's soft and silky.

In weaving, nothing works better than a woolen-spun weft for warm, lightweight fabric. Woolen-spun yarns aren't usually used for warp because they aren't strong enough to withstand the abrasion of the weaving process. (One exception is attenuated long draw; see page 75.) Fabrics with a woolen-spun weft can be napped with a brush to give the fabric a soft, velvety surface. Depending on the fiber, woolen-spun yarns can also make wonderful felt. Some fabrics, such as Harris Tweed, depend on woolen yarn's ability to felt, locking the fibers in place to create a rugged, warm, and lightweight cloth.

FIBER

To make a perfect woolen yarn, choose a fiber with a high crimp, more than seven crimps per inch.  The fiber should be 2½ inches (6.5 centimeters) or shorter; cut it to an appropriate length if necessary. (Contrary to popular belief, scissors are a spinner's tool.) Longer fibers will straighten themselves out, creating a more worsted effect during the drafting process. Cashmere, camel down, any down-breed sheep, Merino, cotton, silk noil, bison, and yak all respond beautifully to being spun woolen. Medium breeds, such as Corriedale, are perfect for woolen spinning.

Many commercial blends such as Merino/cashmere and Merino/yak are sold as prepared top for worsted spinning. Give them a quick wash in hot water to reactivate the crimp; they'll spin woolen beautifully. Roving prepared at small carding mills isn't combed and, if the fiber has the right crimp and length, should be good for woolen spinning.

Unlike fibers for worsted spinning, woolen fibers don't need to be strong. They

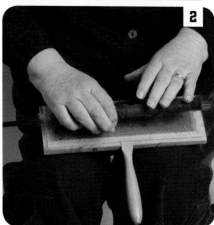

also don't have to be the same length or micron. The finishing technique used for woolen-spun yarns and fabrics actually stabilizes tender and broken fibers.

PREPARATION

The ideal preparation for woolen spinning deliberately crosses the fibers as much as possible. Use either handcards or a drumcarder  to open up the fibers and distribute them evenly. Take the fiber off the handcards by making rolags or punis. A puni (a term commonly used with cotton) is more firmly packed than a rolag, which is airy.

Handcards come in all different shapes and sizes. Just like wool combs, try a few to see what fits both your hand and the type of spinning that you like to do. If you're interested in fine fibers like cotton, cashmere, or bison, cotton handcards (which are very fine) are a good investment.

Carding machines do exactly what handcards do—they just do it faster. A wide variety of carders exist, differing in what they do best and offering many preparation options. For production, try an electric carder. You'll find that rolling the batt from end to end after it's off the carder increases the number of crosses.

WOOLEN DRAW

Also called long draw, true woolen is the fastest of the draws, and I find it the most elegant to watch. Woolen draw lets twist enter the web before the fibers are attenuated. When the twist enters the fiber, it's rotating, like a whirlpool of energy. Because the fiber isn't under tension, the twist swirls the fiber around, letting the fibers tangle together. If you look at woolen yarn under a microscope, you'll see that the ends of the fiber have a tendency to lie perpendicular to the yarn, forming a mesh that traps air efficiently. This arrangement of fibers also lets yarns such as angora have a halo and woolen fabrics be napped.

To spin true woolen, let the twist enter the web of unspun fiber. **4** Move the web (fiber supply) back gently and smoothly, away from the wheel, letting the twist run evenly through the fibers. **5** As your fiber

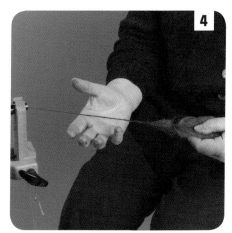
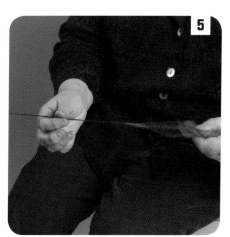

hand moves back, tighten your drafting fingers so that no additional twist goes into the web. You'll feel in the fiber hand when the twist starts to decrease; the diameter of the yarn will also decrease and the web will feel much less stable. Stop drafting back and quickly let in a little more twist. **6** Work this way as far back as your fiber arm feels comfortable, adding a little twist, like glue, to keep the web together. **7** Then, in one smooth motion, let all the yarn move forward onto the bobbin. Start again, letting twist enter the

web, drafting back in a pinch, release, pull back motion.

When you're spinning woolen, don't be alarmed about breaks. Woolen-spun yarn is delicate. Simply rely on a good woolen join. Lay about 10 inches (25.5 centimeters) of spun yarn over the unspun fiber and let the twist transfer from the wheel to the spun yarn and from the spun yarn to the fiber. When the twist reaches the fiber, draw back and begin a woolen draw. **8**

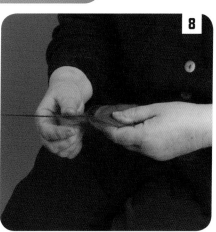

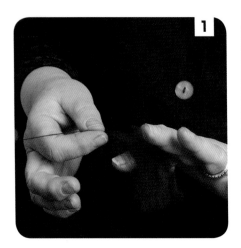

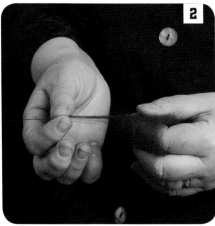

Problems, Pitfalls, and Helpful Hints

- If woolen spinning is new to you, you may have some trouble controlling the yarn diameter. A common problem for woolen spinners is that the yarn becomes thinner and thinner until it finally breaks. Check to make sure that you're letting enough twist enter the web. The more twist, the thicker the yarn; the less twist, the thinner the yarn. Sometimes, opening your hand up a little more or moving the point where you hold the fiber supply back away from the yarn being formed can help as well.
- If you have the heart and the hand of a worsted spinner, be sure you let that twist go into the web. Open the fingers of your drafting hand and count three foot-beats of twist before you start to draw back.
- Check to make sure the hand holding the fiber isn't clenched. You need to hold that fiber as if it were a baby bird. The fiber needs to move out of the web smoothly.
- Because woolen yarn is generally low twist and a bit fragile, don't try to pull the yarn off the bobbin with the brake band on.

- Remember which hook you're on in case you lose an end. Move hooks often when you spin woolen so that the bobbin fills very evenly.
- Let the singles set on the bobbin for twenty-four hours or so before you try to ply. The yarn compresses a bit and is easier to pull off the bobbins.

Semiworsted, Semiwoolen, and Everything Between

By mixing fiber, preparation, and drafting elements, you can create an infinite variety of yarns that have some traits of both worsted and woolen yarns. Almost all yarns fall somewhere on the spectrum between true worsted and true woolen. Whether worsted or woolen traits dominate, choose the combination of techniques and traits that create the kind of yarn you want. The following techniques are some of the most common and useful ways of creating semiworsted and semiwoolen yarns.

SPINNING FROM THE FOLD

Spinning from the fold is a classic example of a method that can be used to produce either a semiwoolen or semiworsted yarn. This drafting method organizes the fibers so that they're bent in half as the twist enters them. To spin a semiworsted yarn over the fold, hold a lock or staple length of fiber over the first finger of your fiber hand. **1** Let the twist catch just at the fold, then draft toward the orifice as you would for a true worsted draw. **2** Just as in a normal worsted draw, be careful to keep the twist from sliding into the fiber folded over your finger.

Use the same type of fiber as for worsted

Having trouble adjusting a double-drive wheel to spin a fine, low-twist single? If you can, change to scotch brake. Because a double drive adjusts the bobbin pulley and the wheel pulley together, it's difficult to get just the right drafting speed. If it's right for drafting back, it buckles winding onto the bobbin. The scotch brake was designed to fix that. If you can't change your wheel, try using a free weight, a common trick spinners used before scotch tension was developed. Tie a line so that it lies over the bobbin and attach a weight (fish weights and washers work well) over the bobbin. Adjust the weight until the yarn pulls on perfectly. (See "A Very Accurate Scotch Tension" by Peter Teal, *Spin·Off* magazine, Winter 2007.) You can also add extra tension on the yarn by resting your finger on it as it winds on.

spinning—long and smooth. I especially like this method for spinning alpaca and llama, which tend either to become little stainless steel wires when twisted too much or to sag and stretch out of shape when spun too loosely. Spinning semiworsted this way produces yarn with an interesting texture and adds loft without making the yarn unstable. The downside is it reduces the yarn's ability to withstand abrasion and, because the fibers are no longer parallel, reduces the luster.

What makes spinning from the fold work differently from true worsted is the way the fibers are organized. Because the fiber is straight but bent in half, the energy of the fiber (remember that fiber always tries to return to its original shape) pushes the ends toward the outside of the yarn as it tries to straighten the bent fiber. It is this pressure that creates the texture and the loft.

This yarn is semiworsted because the twist is entered into attenuated fibers that are mostly straight, then drafted toward the wheel, making yarn with more worsted than woolen characteristics. You could also hold a chunk of batt or roving over your finger, allow twist between your hands, and use a long backward draw to spin from the fold; the resulting yarn would have more woolen characteristics.

Problems, Pitfalls, and Helpful Hints

● One of the drawbacks of spinning from the fold is that the fiber choice is limited. Silk isn't always a good choice, even though it's the very definition of long and silky. Because the fiber is so fine and lacks scales, silk usually collapses inward instead of pushing outward when it's spun using this method. Semiworsted also reduces silk's luster significantly. The yarn will still have a wonderful hand, but it will look a bit more like cotton than silk. Most manufactured fibers have the same limitation, but the technique does work well with bamboo.

● Try to have your fiber well organized before you start spinning. If you're using already prepared fiber, break off staple-length pieces ahead of time. Separate fleece into locks.

ATTENUATED LONG DRAW

The attenuated long draw is for fibers that are too short and fine to be spun worsted comfortably. It's used to produce a yarn that has many of worsted's qualities. The yarn is strong enough to use as a warp yarn and has good stitch definition. This method decreases the felting and fulling possibilities.

Hold a cloud of very fine fiber gently in your fiber hand. Follow the steps for a classic long draw until you have about 18 inches (46 centimeters) drafted out. **3** Tighten both hands and give a sharp tug so that your hands move away from one another. Yarn will magically form between your fingers. Open the drafting hand and let in twist a bit at a time until the yarn has the amount you want. Move your drafting hand up the yarn, twisting and smoothing it as you go to create an even surface. **4 5** When the yarn has enough twist, feed it onto the wheel and start again. Although this technique uses the woolen techniques of twist between the hands, a long drafting area, and carded fibers, it can transform the shortest and fluffiest fibers into durable yarn.

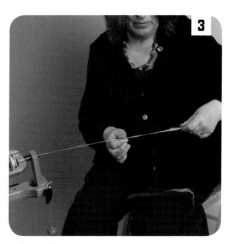

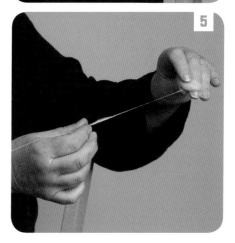

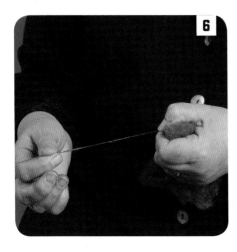
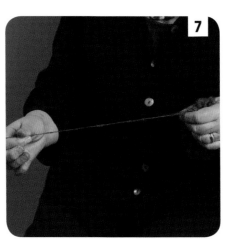

WORSTED DRAW
WITH WOOLEN FIBERS

This semiwoolen method uses loose crossed fibers as true woolen does, and the twist enters them without tension before drafting. **6** However, the fibers are pulled forward toward the wheel after the twist is entered, not away from the wheel as with woolen. **7** This forward draft stretches the fibers and aligns them slightly. The attenuation of the fibers as twist enters adds extra strength, distributes twist more evenly, and gives a more clearly defined knitted stitch.

Semiwoolen spinning puts more structure in the yarn, but the fibers still enter the drafting zone crossed, and the finished yarn behaves more like woolen than worsted. It will wear well, but will be slightly heavier than a true woolen. Semiwoolen will not felt as readily as a true woolen and will have less halo.

Semiwoolen is one of the most common methods of spinning. A variation on woolen, this much-loved draw is an excellent way to spin cashmere, bison, and other short crimpy fibers that need a bit more structure, especially to make a knitting yarn. Much lighter and less defined than a worsted yarn, semiwoolen-spun yarn has more strength and stitch definition than pure woolen. Like woolen, semiwoolen works best with fibers shorter than two and a half inches and with more than seven crimps per inch. Fibers such as angora and cashmere can easily be spun semiwoolen from a teased handful of fiber. You can spin a good semiwoolen yarn from many commercial fine wool and wool blend tops, especially if you reactivate the crimp before you start spinning (see page 71).

WORSTED

- Firm stitch definition
- Withstands abrasion
- Uses fleece longer than 2½ inches with less than 7 crimps per inch
- Little change when washed
- Structure is in the single (overspin and underply)
- Twist enters straight, tensioned fibers
- Prepared by combing
- Uses long fibers (Romney, flax, silk)
- Felts (contracts) in fabric
- Lustrous
- Strong
- Cool

WOOLEN

- Soft stitch definition
- Abrades
- Fiber shorter than 2½ inches with more than 7 crimps per inch
- Dramatic change when washed
- Structure is in the ply (underspin and overply)
- Twist enters deliberately crossed fibers
- Prepared by carding
- Uses highly crimped fibers (Merino, cotton, yak)
- Fulls (expands) in fabric
- Matte finish
- Not strong
- Warm

The two main drafting "families," woolen and worsted.

Problems, Pitfalls, and Helpful Hints

- When you spin semiwoolen, be careful to make short, quick draws. If you let too much twist into the web, especially if you're using prepared top, the twist will work like glue and make it difficult to draft out the fiber.
- Letting too much twist into the web before you draft forward can also be the cause of uneven spinning. With too much twist in the web, the temptation is to pull hard to release the fiber, creating a large slub.

Intentional Slub Draw

You can use the intentional slub draw to produce a rhythmically textured yarn. It's one of the most useful singles used to create a variety of novelty yarns. Most spinners remember how annoying it was to spin a slubbed yarn accidentally and how easily the slubs appeared; the only difficulty in spinning intentional slubs is overcoming all the training it took to avoid them. (If you want to teach beginners how to avoid accidental slubs, give them a project for which they need to spin slubs on purpose. After making slubs on purpose, most spinners will understand how not to make them as well.)

Intentional slubs do differ from accidental slubs: they occur at regular intervals. They also are firmly spun. Curiously, slubs naturally occur in a mathematically perfect pattern. That's because the length of the slub is related to the length of the fibers—the shorter the fibers, the shorter the interval between the slubs; the longer the fibers, the longer the intervals.

FIBER AND PREPARATION

Slub yarns can be made from most tops and roving. Cashmere slubs, wool slubs, silk slubs, fine wool slubs, cotton slubs—the list is endless. It is not possible to make a slub yarn unless the fibers have been processed into top, roving, or batts; it won't work with airy rolags or unprocessed locks.

SPINNING INTENTIONAL SLUBS

Attach the fiber to the leader yarn on your bobbin. Set your wheel so that it pulls the yarn on firmly. Draft forward as if for worsted and pull the fiber out of the web until it's nearly transparent. **1 2** It should make you feel nervous, as if it were going to break; leave just enough fiber to keep the thread continuous. Keep your fingers on the fiber and the twist in front of your fingers. Slide your fingers back to the hand that holds the fiber. As with traditional worsted spinning, the twist should follow your fingers back. (Don't yank your drafting hand back suddenly, or the slub will peel off instead of being smooth and integrated.) **3** When your fingers are back at the web, draft another length and pull just to the breaking point.

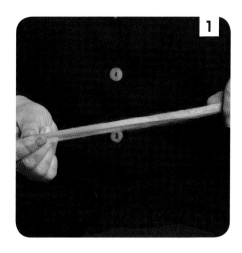

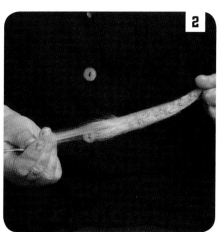

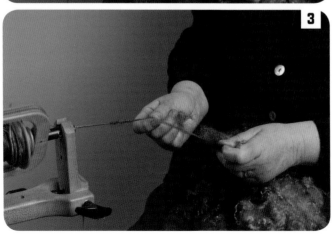

Bouclé Draw

In my studio, we call this "wolf" yarn—not because of its wild and fearless qualities but because its sales have kept the wolf from the studio door for the last thirty-five years. It's very strong—I use it for warp—and incredibly lightweight. This draw uses the basic principles of bouclé making (holding some of the fiber out from the yarn at a 90-degree angle), but uses them on fiber instead of yarn.

Choose a fiber that's suitable for worsted spinning: washed but not carded mohair, raw angora, Romney locks. Gently tease it apart, leaving the lock structure still somewhat intact. **1** Use the pulley that draws in the fastest on your wheel, usually the one with the largest diameter (see page 85). If you have a bobbin-driven wheel, it will work very well for this technique.

Start the wheel and attach the bobbin leader to the fiber. Hold the fiber loosely in the fiber hand. **2** With the thumb and forefinger of your drafting hand, reach over and loosen a clump of fiber from the fiber hand. **3** With your back two fingers, tuck some of the clump into your palm, then use these fingers and the base of your thumb to spin a fine, tight single out of the fiber stashed in your palm. **4** (Imagine that you're spinning as usual, but between your back fingers and palm instead of your forefinger and the tip of your thumb; it may help to practice this part before moving to the next step.) At the same time, pull the loose fiber out with your thumb and your forefinger at a 90-degree angle to the finely spun yarn. **5** Relax the fiber slightly so that it catches and wraps around the fine thread in textured bouclé-style loops. **6** Let the wrapped length feed on and repeat.

The process looks deceptively easy, but it isn't; it takes some spinning skill to keep all the parts going. But it is fun! It may help to think of it as spinning two yarns at once, one thin and even, one wispy and textured. To get a feel for it, try using a commercially spun thread for the thin-and-even component.

A production spinner needs to find a yarn that is not only profitable but also challenging, structurally sound, and fun to work with. After all these years, I still find bouclé yarn to be all those things. In the studio, I treat this yarn like chicken soup stock: the singles become an ever-changing variety of yarns.

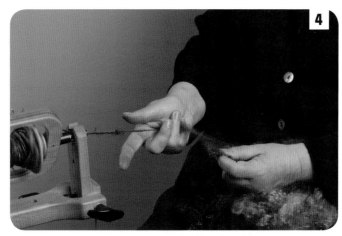

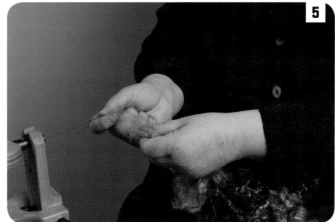

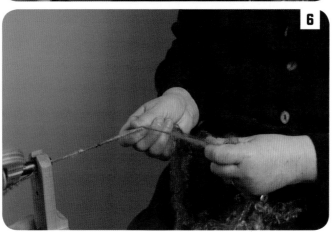

CHAPTER SIX

plied yarns, cables, and novelty yarns

PLIED YARNS ARE THE workhorses of the textile world. They are strong, durable, and most of all they are dependable. They wear well and are stable and easy to handle. Plied yarns are highly efficient structures.

The word "ply" has several different sources, all with similar meanings. The medieval English word plien and French plier both mean "to fold." In Latin, it is derived from the word pilcare, which means "to braid." Although we will never know the exact evolution of spinning terms and techniques, many examples of yarns or marks that yarn made on prehistoric artifacts show both braided and plied yarns. Currently, many textile researchers believe that braided yarns came first and were replaced by plied yarns as spinning skills developed.

Early Egyptian tomb drawings show spinners folding thread to make a plied yarn: one spinner walks away from the other, holding out the spun single. Using this method, when they have drawn out the length needed for warp thread, the second spinner inserts a stick, and the remaining thread is drawn out until it matches the length of the first thread. The second spinner then uses the stick to apply twist to the thread. In the medieval silk city of Bursa, in Turkey, I've watched men make high-twist silk warp threads from reeled silk for handknotted silk carpets in this same timeless way, one warp thread at a time. In modern day spinning workshops, you see a variation of this folded-ply method, a spinner walking a strand of yarn across a room and folding it back on itself to see what the finished yarn will be like.

In the textile world (both for handspinners and in textile industries), a plied yarn is defined as two or more singles twisted together with a reverse twist. Many yarns consist of two singles wound together with the same twist as the single; they are still singles. It's the reverse twist that changes the yarn to a plied yarn. We use the word single (or singles) to refer to a yarn with a single twist; a plied yarn is a yarn with two directions of twist, a cable is a yarn with three (or more) directions of twist. Because of this important distinction, avoid using the term "single-ply" to describe a yarn.

Why Ply?

I'm a firm believer in plying as a spinner's default position—do it unless you have a really good reason not to.

STRENGTH

A plied yarn is stronger than the singles it's made from, both in tensile strength (the ability to withstand weight and stretching) and resistance to abrasion (friction). One of the first principles of textile design is that a yarn made from many strands of fiber held together by twist energy is stronger than the individual fibers without twist. By the same principle, that strength increases exponentially with plying. Plying adds another layer and direction of twist, binding many more fibers together. In the ply structure, more individual fibers are covered and protected from abrasion, light, and chemical damage.

CONSISTENCY

Plying is one of the best ways to produce a consistent yarn. A consistent yarn doesn't necessarily mean a smooth, even-surfaced yarn or even one with the same diameter or number of plies throughout the skein. It means a yarn in which all the traits, good and bad, are regularly distributed throughout the skein—even one that's consistently inconsistent. Consistency is important because it lets you create a fabric or garment that won't suffer unintended changes in size caused by diameter change in the yarn, in texture caused by changes in fiber preparation, or in color caused by changes in fiber lots.

EFFICIENCY

Although you can see that a yarn is consistent by looking at it, important but invisible traits will make an enormous difference in what a yarn can and can't do. For instance, a plied yarn occupies more space than the singles that made it. The energy from the opposing twists lets the yarn relax and open up without losing its strength. When you knit or weave, the finished piece will weigh less if you use a plied yarn rather than a single of the same diameter. You never save time by not plying if you use the yarn yourself because using a single requires more yarn. You only save time by not plying when you're spinning yarn to sell.

STABILITY

One of the most important first principles of textiles is that all fiber returns to its original shape. Singles have a wild and abundant energy. They're always moving, trying to untwist. Plied yarns are more stable because the twist energy in the singles is counteracted by the ply twist. Think of plied yarns as two pillars that fall toward each other and meet. Their motion stops, and each supports the one opposite. They're still and secure.

KNITTING AND WEAVING PERFORMANCE

Yarns come in a wide range of plies, but the most important difference for yarn designers to understand is the difference between a two-ply and a multi-ply (three, four, five, or even more). Two-ply yarns have a grittier, more textured surface than yarns made with more plies and, like singles, two-ply yarns produce a less polished surface. Two-ply yarns have a serrated edge that lets them do what they do best: hold their space and keep the threads apart.

In knitting, when you make the loop to form a stitch, a two-ply yarn moves away from the center of the stitch; a three-ply yarn, on the other hand, folds into the center of the stitch, filling it up. The characteristics of a two-ply yarn enhance the lace-knitting technique, making each stitch more defined. In weaving, a two-ply yarn locks the fabric in place (see page 131); the rounder surface of a three-ply yarn lets the warp and weft yarns slip by one another, making denser, heavier cloth. In weaving, use a two-ply as your default yarn.

Multi-ply yarns are a knitter's joy. If you worry that your knitting tension isn't consistent, try switching to a multi-ply yarn. Often, it's the way the yarn opens up that makes knitting appear uneven. An uneven appearance is frequently a problem for silky fibers such as Merino top, alpaca, and kid mohair blends. Multi-plies have a smooth, round surface. Whenever a smooth surface is necessary to the design of your work, the more plies, the better. Aran and Guernsey patterns are a good example. The roundness of traditional five- or six-ply yarns ensures a smooth, almost carved surface for the cable pattern.

VISUAL APPEAL

Plying lets handspinners create a rich variety of color and textures. Most novelty yarns, such as bouclés and encased yarns, are based on plying techniques (see page 87). Plying is a wonderful way to create unusual color effects, letting a spinner use color like a painter. You can also create fiber blends by plying; this is especially useful for fibers that would be lovely together but require totally different spinning methods. Rather than struggling to spin short, crimpy yak with long, straight silk—an unrewarding task—spin each separately and ply them together to make a wonderful yarn with the best qualities of both fibers.

How to Ply

Plying with a wheel actually uses a slight variation on the early Egyptian folding method. The wheel lets you make a much, much longer length of yarn than you could by folding, and it's of course much faster. I often hear my spinning students say, "But it takes sooo long!" Truly, it doesn't. Plying only takes about one-third of the time it took to spin the original singles, and plied yarn (among all its other advantages) will make much more fabric than singles will.

When yarn is plied, the twist enters all the singles at once. For a four-ply yarn, all the singles are drafted together at the same time. A yarn made from two two-plies twisted together in the opposite direction would be a completely different type of yarn called a four-strand cable. A two-ply yarn with a singles added to it in another plying pass is called a crepe or cord yarn. It has wonderful characteristics, but it isn't a three-ply, nor will it do the job for which three-ply was created.

PREPARING FOR CONSISTENCY

The surest way to make a consistent yarn is to spin all the singles before you start to ply (or at least as many as you can bear to). Have as many bobbins as you possibly can, or transfer your yarn to cheaper storage bobbins with a bobbin winder. Take a good look at the spun bobbins; look for changes in diameter or amount of twist, any difference in color distribution, or anything that makes one a little different from the rest.

If you have a bobbin where the single is off slightly, add a bit from that bobbin to every skein as you ply. Spread evenly throughout your whole project, you won't notice any difference at all. When I ply, I rotate my bobbins and use about a quarter bobbin each time, changing bobbins using a simple splice (see page 87). Spinning just two bobbins and then plying them together can produce uneven yarn, no matter how well you spin, because the inconsistencies are concentrated rather than spread out.

Rewinding your bobbins also makes a difference in the consistency of the finished yarn. While the singles are being rewound, the twist can move freely back and forth like water in the length between the bobbins. This movement allows the twist to distribute itself more evenly. Set up the bobbin winder at a distance from the bobbin being wound off to let the twist be redistributed. When you rewind from a bobbin on a wheel, remove the tension from the bobbin. As you wind onto the new bobbin, guide it back and

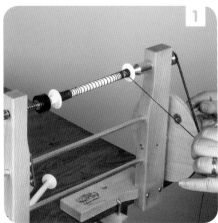

For the same reason that I mix the singles, I avoid plying from the inside and outside of a center-pull ball; it creates more problems than the extra work to wind your bobbins into separate balls. First, plying from the inside and the outside concentrates the inconsistencies in fiber preparation and drafting instead of spreading them out. Second, it creates a situation in which one single goes one way and the other is in reverse. It's not a question of right and left twist—the twist runs the same way when viewed from either end—but of the "grain" of the yarn.

Similar to the grain in paper and fabric or in the direction of top, the grain of the singles results from the direction of the drafting during the spinning process. When the grain of the singles isn't matched up in the plying process, the finished yarn has a much greater tendency to pill and isn't as stable. (These drawbacks aren't a problem for quick samples and small projects that don't need to have a long life span or withstand a lot of wear.) Finally, for fine or high-twist singles, you may find it harder to keep order. I seem unable to prevent the inside of the ball from collapsing on itself and creating a tightly tangled snarl, usually destroying about a third of my fine singles (and requiring a lot more time than rewinding in the first place).

forth to wind it evenly, like thread on a sewing machine bobbin. **1** A spinner can't make such even bobbins on a wheel except with a device such as a WooLee Winder. Rewinding makes plying a lot smoother and faster. I don't rewind for textured yarns, but I do for all even yarns and especially for lace yarns.

ARRANGING BOBBINS

Before you start plying, you need to find some method to support your bobbins of spun singles. Many wheels have storage racks or rods for bobbins on the wheel, and it's tempting to use them to ply. However, with the exception of Louet wheels, which have a well-designed plying frame, try to resist. The storage racks hold the bobbins at an awkward angle, making it difficult to draw the singles off the bobbins evenly.

The piece of equipment used to hold the bobbins is called a lazy kate. Kates come in a wide variety of styles and price ranges. Some are quite basic and others are refined examples of the woodworker's art. What I look for in a kate is stability. I want it to stay where I put it and not tip over or drag along the floor. Some kates are just plain heavy; I have one that weighs 15 pounds (6.8 kilograms), and it definitely stays put. Some are designed to be clamped to a surface, and I've found that a furniture clamp will hold most others in place. I prefer to have the bobbins at a forty-five degree angle because it lets yarn be pulled off more smoothly. **2**

If you don't have a kate, you can easily make one. When I travel, I use an inexpensive plastic basket and a set of old metal straight knitting needles. A cardboard box works just as well—use the knitting needles to pop holes in the sides and suspend your bobbins on the needles. Making your own has one huge advantage over most that you buy: you can have as many bobbins as you need. Most traditional kates limit you to three or four bobbins, but with a cardboard-box kate, you can make wonderful five-ply gansey yarns or ten-ply cashmere.

When you put your bobbins on the kate, make sure that the yarn pulls off all of them in the same direction. If you don't, it can create a dreadful tangle. It must make a difference if the yarn is pulled from over the top or underneath bobbins held horizontally, because everything in spinning has an effect on the yarn, but I haven't noticed a difference—yet! To be on the safe side, make a choice and do it consistently.

CHOOSING A PULLEY

Choosing the proper pulley for plying depends on the type of singles you spin and the type of plying twist you want. Use a bigger pulley to ply a classic worsted yarn than you use to spin the singles, and use a smaller pulley to ply a classic woolen yarn than you use to spin the singles. The difference in the pulley size used for plying is due to the nature of the singles. A worsted yarn's structure is all in the singles; it needs only enough ply twist to balance the yarn. Using a large pulley will put in less ply twist. A classic woolen yarn, however, has next to no structure in the singles. It relies on the ply twist to give it structure and stability, and a smaller pulley adds more twist.

If your yarn, like most, is a variation on these two types, then think of the function of the yarn you want to produce and let

that guide you. Even though a sock yarn is spun worsted, it might need more structure, so use the same or a smaller pulley than you used for the singles. A good blanket weft yarn will need softer plying twist, even though you have likely spun it woolen, so try a bigger pulley.

If your wheel doesn't have any choice of pulleys, apply a bit more pressure on the drive band (or tighten it) for worsted, and apply a little less pressure on the drive band (or loosen it) for woolen. These adjustments will change the drafting-in speed of your wheel; more tension means faster drafting-in speed, producing less plying twist, and less tension means a slower drafting-in speed, resulting in more plying twist.

HANDLING THE YARN

To get ready to ply, organize your singles. Place them on your leg, choosing the side that feels natural to you. I'm a right-handed spinner and hold my singles in my left

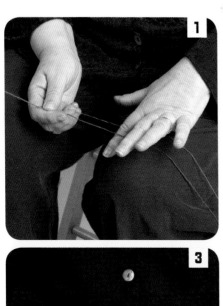
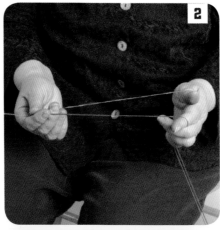
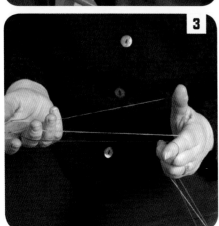
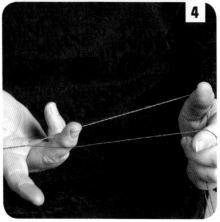

Here's how I position my hands for a simple two-ply. First, using the hand that would usually hold the fiber and approaching the singles from above, slip your first finger between the two singles. Your thumb will be on the outside of the threads toward the inside of your leg. **1** Rotate your hand toward the outside of your leg so that your thumb slips under the first thread. Lift your hand and tilt it back. **2** (If you're a knitter, the position may be familiar; it's the one you use for a long-tail Continental cast-on.) When I do multiple plies, I use this same method, adding another finger for each extra ply. **3** Using this method, I can comfortably spin a five-ply.

With your drafting hand, place your middle finger under the strands and lift it through the V that they form, with the palm of your hand facing you. **4** This finger will make sure that the twist enters all the strands at the same time. Your thumb and forefinger are free to pinch and draft as they would normally when spinning with a short draw. If you need to let go, let go with this hand, the drafting hand. The tensioning hand is the one that keeps everything in order and prevents chaos. Pretend it's glued in place—don't move it back and forth. Failing to keep steady tension with this hand is the major cause of tangles and will cause the bobbins to lash back on themselves.

hand, the same hand in which I would hold my fiber. I use my right hand, the hand I draft with, to manage the twist and correct the singles as I ply.

The way I hold my hands when I ply is an old British style. I like this method because it gives me amazing control over the singles, but there really isn't a right or wrong way to hold your hands. If you have a method that feels comfortable, lets you keep the same tension on all the singles, and keeps the twist entering all of them at the same time, you needn't make a change.

THE MOTIONS OF PLYING

Use your drafting hand (or your foot) to start your wheel. Remember to go in the opposite direction from how the singles were spun. Place your fingers back in the plying position and use your thumb and forefinger to grasp the singles and pull forward toward the wheel's orifice. Keep the back hand steady. When your fingers reach the orifice, draw them smoothly back toward the tensioning hand. The twist will follow your fingers back. **5** The faster you move your fingers, the less ply twist you'll have in your yarn. The slower you move your hands, the more ply twist you'll have.

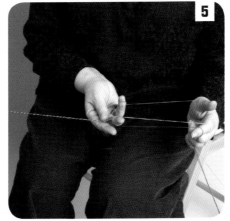

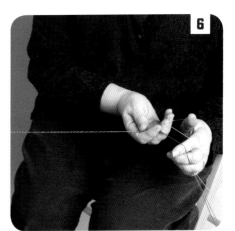

When you reach your back hand, clamp the thumb and forefinger of your drafting hand so that the twist can't go any farther **6** and feed all the plied yarn onto the wheel. **7** Traditionally, the yarn is fed onto the wheel in half the time that it was drafted out. Keep that back hand steady—don't move it—and the next length to be plied will be drawn out evenly and smoothly. Remember to change hooks or move the yarn guide often while plying because the bobbin fills up quite quickly.

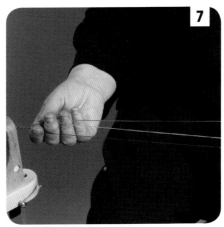

Few spinners make perfect singles, especially when spinning a woolen-type yarn, but when you ply, thin and thick places often merge. Plying gives you an opportunity to correct areas in the singles that are overspun or underspun. You do so with the drafting hand. Use your thumb to apply pressure on slubs before they enter the twisting zone. You can also adjust areas with too much twist by lifting them with your forefinger to let twist run out of the single before it reaches the twisting zone. If you have an occasional large slub or especially thin place, just break it out of your yarn and rejoin with a simple splice. You don't need to leave any accidental faults in your plied yarn; taking them out is simply good spinning sense.

To splice yarns while plying, lay the new end between the two strands connected to the bobbin and hold it with the broken strand. **8** Let the twist join the strands together and tuck in the ends. **9**

To count or not to count? This is probably the second-most frequently asked question about plying (right after "Do I have to

ply?"). What you would be counting is the number of foot-beats for each length of yarn. Each time you treadle the wheel, you put in the same number of twists over the same length of yarn; that number depends on your wheel and the pulley you're using. When you count, you pull the same length of singles forward every time and add the same amount of twist.

Think of counting as a plying aid rather than a necessity. I'm not likely to count every foot-beat in 2 pounds of yarn. However, counting will help you establish a rhythm when you start a new type of yarn, and it's a good practice to check now and then to see if you're still on track, especially when you start a new bobbin. Remember that one of the aims of plying is to produce a consistent twist throughout all the skeins in your project, and counting can help you do it.

CHOOSING THE AMOUNT OF PLYING TWIST

Are you unsure how many twists per inch will be right for your project? Use your threading hook on your singles to test what a balanced yarn looks and feels like. **10** I learned this clever trick, which has saved

me from many unfortunate yarns, from Celia Quinn, the brilliant spinner from Alaska. If the yarn that you get is the yarn you want, count the number of twists per inch, then spin the rest of the singles with a similar twist per inch. If the yarn isn't what you want—either too much twist or too little twist when plied—change the singles. Even if you've spun a lot of singles already, you can add or reduce twist. Simply run the singles back through the wheel—in the direction it was spun to increase the twist, or the opposite direction to release twist. Once you know what a balanced yarn looks like, add or subtract twist where necessary so the yarn creates a balanced fabric.

It's the twist in the singles—not the ply twist—that sets how a yarn will balance when it's plied. If you're not sure what's making your yarn unbalanced, take a look at the direction of the twist in the skein. That twist is trying to counteract the extra twist in your yarn. It's twisting in the opposite direction from the overtwist. If the skein is twisting to the left, it has too much right twist, and vice versa. If the ply twist has caused the problem, you can correct it

just as you corrected the twist in the singles, by running it through the wheel to either tighten or release twist.

No matter how experienced a spinner you are, you'll ply in the wrong direction at least once. When (not if) this happens, take a deep breath, stay calm, and simply run the whole bobbin back in the correct plying direction; if you've skeined it off, put it on a swift and spin it back from there. You'll see the yarn snap apart, the twist disappear, and the correct twist be entered properly. With a wash, you'll never be able to tell it wasn't plied correctly the first time.

Although the plyback test is a good way to check your yarn on the fly, bear in mind that the only way to know for sure is to sample. Complete a small skein, then finish it and swatch it in its finished state.

Because singles may spend time sitting on the bobbin waiting to be plied, twist in the singles may settle and become dormant, so plying yarn to look just like your plyback test may not give you the results you expect. If you have singles that have been resting for days or more, you may find it useful to ply a short sample, then wash it and let it

on balanced yarn

I have found in my work that singles and plied yarns that balance beautifully in the skein usually fail to balance beautifully in the fabric, especially if knitted. And how could they? Everything we do transforms the yarn. Yarn that is balanced straight off the wheel will lose significant twist when it is washed and again when it is wound, and twist will be added or subtracted as it is knitted or woven. I've learned to aim for yarn that will have the correct twist to carry through the process with the energy to make beautiful, stable cloth. There is no shortcut or magic formula for finding which twist makes the perfect yarn. Sample, and pay attention to what happens to your yarn during the process of making cloth.

dry unweighted to get a clear picture of the amount of plying twist you want to use.

Cabled Yarns

Cabled fibers are everywhere in the modern world. They are the materials of construction: metal cables for bridges, steel cables that make the cords in tires, corded yarns woven into industrial mesh for indestructible carpeting. If plied yarns are the workhorses of the textile world, cables are the industrial-grade trucks.

But cables are spun for beauty's sake as well. Decorative cable yarns have been used for clothing, basket trim, and animal and human adornment. Ceremonial yarns made with everything from rabbit fur and sinew to hummingbird down and eagle feathers use cabling techniques.

When I first looked carefully at cabled yarns, I was convinced that they weren't spun at all but knitted or braided on some clever modern machine. I was in for a wonderful surprise. Cables aren't modern inventions that involve machinery; humans have been spinning cables since prehistoric times. Then as now, cables were used in construction. They lashed rafts together, they supported bridges, and they were the cordage on boats. Early fishermen made fishnets and weirs with them; hunters made traps and snowshoes.

Cables have made the modern explosion of novelty yarns possible. Bouclés, brushed wools, mohair novelties, and encasement yarns are just a few examples of designer yarns that depend on knowledge of how cables work. (For more on novelty yarns, see page 92.)

A cable is a yarn made when two or more plied yarns are spun together in the direction opposite to the ply twist. Cables can be made from yarn with the prime singles spun either to the left or the right. Many yarns are compound cables, made by adding an unbalancing twist to two or more cabled yarns and spinning them together with a reverse twist (opposite from the way they were cabled). The formula remains the same, but the yarns will behave differently.

You might think that two two-ply yarns "plied" together make a four-ply because there are four singles in the yarn. But what they make is a four-strand cable, and what it can do makes it as different from a plied yarn as a plied yarn is from a single.

WHY CABLE?

One of the most important characteristics of a cable is its strength. Just like plied yarns, cables are governed by the principle that a yarn made from many strands of fiber held together by twist energy is stronger than the set of individual fibers without twist. And just as plying increases a yarn's strength exponentially, cabling increases the strength exponentially again. Making a cable also redistributes the twist tension in different directions and in three separate layers, increasing the yarn's tensile strength.

The three layers of twist also mean that even more area of the singles is covered, protecting the fiber from both abrasion and ultraviolet damage. Some cables dramatically increase the elasticity of the yarn, giving any garment made with them more memory, which will help the garment maintain its shape and be more durable.

Cables are extremely stable yarns. The greatest amount of twist is in the middle step, making cables balance beautifully; if they don't hang in a perfect loop, they probably need to be redone. Because the yarn is so well balanced, a cabled yarn lies still, not distorting fabric when knitted or woven in any direction. One joy of working with cables is that they rarely tangle, and when they do they're easily separated.

This hardworking yarn also has a frivolous side; cables aren't limited to just producing classic knitting and weaving yarns. By changing the weight, texture, and color of the different cable components, you can create an endless variety of yarns for knitting. Direction of twist can be mixed as well; bouclés, for instance, have one single spun to the right and one single spun to the left. When these yarns are plied together, one yarn tightens and one yarn loosens.

And then there's the beauty factor. Many cables are beautiful enough to wear by themselves or to use for embellishment. They make effective trims as well as great buttons and other closures. No matter which textile techniques you use, you can rely on cables to create beautiful and unusual cloth.

CABLED YARNS IN FINISHED CLOTH

As a weaving yarn, cables can be used for both warp and weft. Because they're strong and resist tangling, cables are a pleasure to use in a warp. Even quite textured yarns formed by cabling are easy to handle. Used in a mixed warp, a cable will form a length-wise rib, creating an interesting surface texture. In bands in the weft, a cabled yarn has a similar effect, creating a pattern of raised ribs across the fabric. Using cables interspersed in both the warp and the weft produces a series of textured "window panes" in the fabric. When a cable is used for the entire cloth, both warp and weft, a curious thing happens: instead of producing a highly textured cloth, using cables (especially four-strand cables) produces a smooth, silky, lustrous cloth with a surface that resembles a complex satin weave.

In knitting, cables have many uses. Because of their long-wearing nature and the satin-smooth knitted surface they produce, cables are a wonderful choice for a sock yarn. Their smooth surface is also perfect for knits where shaping is a major design component.

Cables react differently depending on which direction the singles were initially spun. Although this principle is equally true for weaving, basketry, and crochet, it's especially noticeable in knitting. If you knit in the Continental style, spinning the singles to the left results in a cable that loosens significantly when it is knitted, while spinning the prime singles to the right results in a cable that tightens when it is knitted.

The reverse is true when you use the English style of knitting. Spinning the singles to the right results in the yarn coming undone. It often looks like two plied yarns on the needle. Spinning the singles to the left results in a yarn that will tighten. Neither of these yarns is right or wrong. Each cable will make a different type of fabric, looser or firmer, depending on the type of knitting and the direction of the original twist.

To understand which type of cable to choose, spin a sample of two identical cable yarns, but reverse the twist direction. Knit these samples at the same gauge to see which will best suit your knitting method, the fiber you're using, and the project you have in mind.

Are there drawbacks to cables? Classic cables (rather than novelty yarns) tend to be denser than plied yarns, so garments made with cabled yarns often weigh a bit more. And, though time should not be a deciding factor, cables involve at least one, and possibly two more complete steps.

MAKE A CABLE

The first step in making a cabled yarn is to spin the singles. Depending on the type of cable you want to make, you'll need two or more bobbins of singles. The most important thing to understand about cables is that the character of the singles, not the plied yarn, determines the cable's twist structure and hand. The firmer the singles, the firmer the cable. Each stage of spinning a cable adds to and magnifies the twist of the last one. It takes little twist to unbal-ance a soft-spun single and much more to unbalance a higher twist single.

The next step is to ply the singles by twisting them together in the opposite direction from the twist in the single. Cables depend on unbalanced plying. If you're an experienced spinner and have worked hard at perfecting a balanced plied yarn, it will take a bit of attention to get the right amount of twist needed to make a yarn cable properly. I find that underplying is the biggest cause of failure in spinning a good cable yarn. As you spin bobbin after bobbin, no matter how technically accurate your wheel might be, the human element is bound to slip in. My hand automatically adjusts for a balanced ply every time my mind wanders. I find that I make a much more technically excellent yarn if I make a balanced ply, then spin the yarn again in the ply direction to add about the same amount of twist again. It introduces exactly the right amount of twist and does it evenly throughout the bobbin. (It also lets me return to my usual spinning habits—reading a bit, daydreaming, and planning the next project.)

Check a length of the plied yarn with a hook, just as you would check the singles' plying twist, to make sure the twist is what you need for the yarn you want to produce. **1** Be sure that the yarn quickly forms a cable. It should "snap" into place as soon as the yarns come in contact with one another. If this isn't the yarn you want, this is the time to correct it by adding or removing twist. You can easily modify singles and plied yarns by adding or removing twist. However, after the cabling step, it's difficult to correct the twist in the yarn.

When you have the necessary twist energy in the plied yarn to make a cable, make sure it stays in the yarn. Either tape the end to the bobbin or tie a knot in it so that it doesn't run out. Twist might also become dormant if you let it sit on the bobbins for several months. If that happens, cable a few lengths of yarn—it will look dreadful—and wash it in hot water with a little soap. The twist should reappear like magic, making your yarn cabled and balanced. If it isn't quite what you want, change it by either re-plying to add more ply twist or reversing the wheel direction to remove ply twist. Sample again until you have the yarn you want.

Once you know you have the correct amount of twist in the plied yarns, put them on a kate and cable them together (to avoid confusion, try not to call this plying, not even to yourself) by turning the wheel in the same direction that the singles were first spun. Be sure to feed it on quite quickly. Don't try to draft the yarns out or guide them into the drafting zone as you would to make a plied yarn; adjust the wheel so that the yarn pulls on faster. Simply feed the yarns onto the wheel. You'll probably need a larger pulley (and a smaller ratio) than the one you used to ply the singles. Remember to move the yarn forward on the hooks often.

Although it's a good place to start, don't stop at a four-strand cable. You can make cables with any combination of plied yarns. Try combining a two-ply and three-ply to make a five-strand cable. Make a six-strand by cabling three two-plies together or by cabling a two-ply and a four-ply together, or by cabling two three-plies together. The possibilities are endless and fascinating.

Problems, Pitfalls, and Helpful Hints

- Before you go too far, check to make sure that the cable is forming properly. It should hang in a perfect loop. **2** If you've fed it on too slowly, it will resemble badly plied yarn. If you didn't add enough twist

at the plying stage, it will be a tangled mess. You can still correct both these problems. To correct the results of the slow feed, for the remaining yarns, feed the cable on very fast. (You might need to increase the drafting-in speed on your wheel.) To correct the low twist, stop cabling and re-ply the bobbins.

- If you've fed all your cable onto the bobbin too slowly and it has come undone, no solution is simple. Try this redesign trick: run the bobbins of cabled yarn back through the wheel one more time in the same direction that you cabled to create an overtwisted cable. Place the cabled yarn on the kate. Using a fine yarn (sewing-thread-weight silk or rayon, fine mohair, or a novelty yarn), bind the cable by twisting the binder and the overtwisted cable in the same direction you originally plied. This technique works best if you started with a right-spun single because it must match up with the commercial thread's direction. Do this really quickly! It will balance out the overtwisted cable and create an interesting, stable compound cable. (See novelty yarns for more about compound cables.)

DESIGNING WITH CABLES

Cable structures are an excellent way to experiment with color and texture effects. They provide endless variations; you could make a cable every day of the year and still not run out of new ways to make yarns using this technique. Try making cables with different fibers, textures, and numbers of plies. You can even cable with commercial yarns. **3** Check to see what direction the commercial yarn is spun, and spin and ply the handspun so they'll be able to cable together.

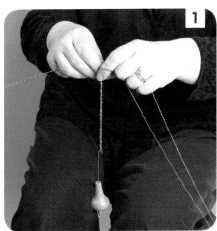

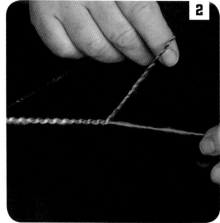

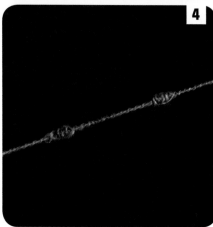

Novelty Yarns

Most novelty yarns come from that unending design source, the happy accident. Like other well-known textile techniques—lace knitting, overshot weaving, and ikat dyeing—most novelty yarns are based on technical "mistakes." They result from taking a common spinning error, understanding it, and repeating it to create a pleasing design. What changes an error into a design feature is intention.

LOOP YARNS

Loop yarns are easily recognizable—all looped and knotted yarns are based on the common plying error of not maintaining equal pressure on the singles. Loop yarns are based on a simple two-ply. You can create variations by using special color effects such as painted rovings, marling, and combining different textures or weights of yarn.

Spiral Yarns

Spiral yarn is deceptively simple to make. Set up as if to make a two-ply yarn, but instead of maintaining equal pressure on both singles, relax one slightly and hold it at a 90-degree angle. **1** The relaxed single will spiral around the taut single. If you're using two different-colored singles, alternate the one that's relaxed to create an interesting color pattern. **2** This yarn can be used as a two-ply, or, with a little extra twist, it makes a delightful cable.

Turkish-Knot Yarns

Begin as for making a spiral. Relax the tension on one single, but instead of holding it steady, let it travel up and down the yarn, wrapping it around the taut single at a 90-degree angle. Go back and forth repeatedly over the same wrapped area, making shorter and shorter passes so it builds up in the middle. **3** When you have the size of knot you want, guide the singles back down the yarn (away from the wheel) and continue plying. Make the knots any size; they don't have to be the same size or occur at the same

interval to be effective. **4** You'll need to cable this yarn to balance the twist, either with itself or with a fine two-ply.

Gimp Yarns

A gimp yarn takes the Turkish-knot yarn to extremes. Just as you did for the Turkish knot, bring the relaxed singles back and forth on the taut singles, but make huge passes up and down the yarn and vary the lengths and number of layers. **5** Imagine scribbling back and forth on the taut singles. **6** You'll need to cable this yarn.

SLUB YARNS

Once you've mastered the intentional slub draw (see page 77), you can use it to create an endless number of beautiful textures. The yarns that this technique produces are a great addition to any textile designer's stash. You can use them for knitting and weaving (both warp and weft). And although their uneven texture makes them difficult to use for traditional stitching, they make a stunning embellishment yarn. Slubs work well with variations of color or fiber (or a combination of both). Here are three yarns you can make based on the slub technique.

Flame Yarns

Flame yarns are made by plying two slubbed singles together. Hold them with even tension. **7** When you start to ply, line up the slubs so that they're offset to create more texture. Ply them in the opposite direction to the spin on the singles. Aim for a fairly balanced yarn if you plan to knit with it or a slightly overtwisted yarn if you plan to use it in a warp. I've used a marled slub in two different color systems. This technique

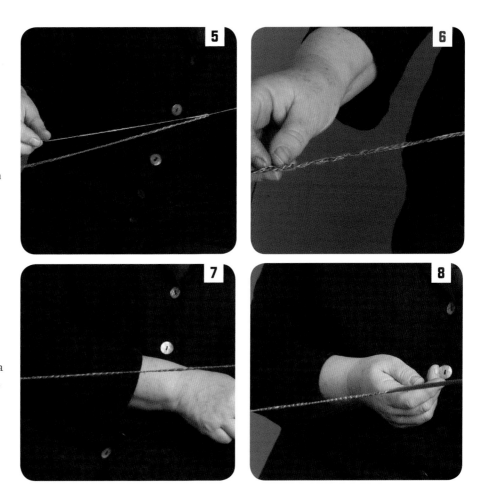

would work well to combine white on white, using a cultivated silk slub and a fine Merino slub, or to combine a thick slubbed yarn with a thin slubbed yarn.

Wave or Rickrack Yarn

You make wave or rickrack yarn by plying a slub singles with a firmly spun smooth singles. **8** I've chosen to use contrasting color variations. Both yarns are spun in the same direction as singles—right—then plied left.

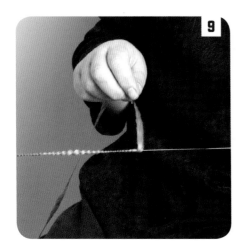

Spiraled Slub Yarn

Although spiraled slub yarn is a little more complex, it's fun to make and a pleasure to use. Spin a bobbin of slub singles to the right and wind a bobbin of any fine commercial two-ply, last spun left. Ply them together to the left, tightening the two-ply and loosening the single. Hold the two-ply tight and straight, and hold the single at right angles to the two-ply. Let the single relax toward the two-ply as you feed it on, as if you were making a simple spiral yarn (see page 92). You should see a thick-and-thin curly loop form as you ply. Keep a firm twist on this yarn, about twice what a balanced yarn should be, because it will need to be cabled.

When you have two bobbins of the plied yarn, cable them together by twisting them to the right. Keep the tension fairly tight on the wheel so that the yarn feeds on quickly. Check to make sure it's balanced; cables should hang in a quiet loop.  This yarn makes a wonderful warp (it's strong enough to tow trucks out of ditches), and it doesn't tangle easily. It's beautiful as either a fine yarn or a bulky yarn. As a knitting yarn, its

knitted surface is highly textured but warm, lightweight, and resistant to pilling.

BOUCLÉ YARNS

The word bouclé comes from the French word *boucler*, which means to buckle or curl. And bouclé yarns certainly do that! They're a weaver's best friend; they let us sett fabric at fewer ends per inch and produce a stable, lightweight cloth. For knitters, bouclés produce a cushy, springy surface that's lush and long-wearing, a great natural alternative to polyester fleece.

Bouclés are based on one yarn last

twisted right and one yarn last twisted left. One sure way is to combine a single and a two-ply. Whether you use handspun, commercially spun, or a combination, both the principles are the same.

I find bouclés endlessly fascinating. They have been my bread-and-butter yarn for more than thirty years, and they solve the worrisome problem of what to do with long, silky fibers. Too often, luster longwools, mohair, and extruded fibers such as bamboo are spun in a classic firm worsted to make them structurally sound. Bouclés are a good solution; they provide an excellent stable structure that holds space in long, low-crimp fibers, adds surface texture, increases volume, and is virtually indestructible. That doesn't mean that fine crimpy yarns aren't great in bouclés—cotton, cashmere, and angora all make great bouclé yarns—but the classic perfect loop requires perfect combed fiber spun worsted firmly. The size and type of loop depend on the lack of crimp in the fiber and the amount of twist in the yarn—softer twist, softer loop; tighter twist, crisper loop.

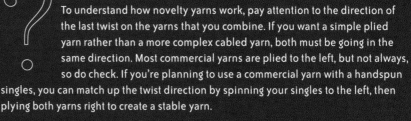

which twist?

To understand how novelty yarns work, pay attention to the direction of the last twist on the yarns that you combine. If you want a simple plied yarn rather than a more complex cabled yarn, both must be going in the same direction. Most commercial yarns are plied to the left, but not always, so do check. If you're planning to use a commercial yarn with a handspun singles, you can match up the twist direction by spinning your singles to the left, then plying both yarns right to create a stable yarn.

Recipe for a Classic Bouclé:

- One yarn spun left, one yarn spun right
- One thick yarn, one thin yarn
- One low-twist yarn, one high-twist yarn

Plying Method:

Set up your yarn as if to ply. I find it easier if I have the yarns on two kates on opposite sides of me. Hold the tightly spun yarn taut and relax the tension on the loose one. Spin in the direction of the most tightly spun yarn (usually the thin one). The looser yarn will form a curl around the tightly spun one. Keep a firm twist in this yarn because it will need to be cabled to hold the loops in place. Use your orifice hook to check whether the yarn will cable and whether the cable is what you want; if not, adjust the twist.

Push-Up Bouclé

Choose two yarns from the bouclé recipe above; I've used painted silk singles and metallic embroidery yarn. Make sure you have enough of the yarn that will make the loops. You'll need significantly more of the loose yarn than of the taut yarn.

Set up your wheel as if to ply and start the wheel. Keep a little less tension on the yarn that will be the loop, in this case the silk. **11** (I let it hang over the back fingers of my fiber hand.) As you ply, use the thumb and forefinger of your drafting hand to push up a length of the yarn into loops on the taut yarn; it will look as if you had gathered it. **12** Continue, keeping it firmly twisted. This yarn needs to be cabled. It can be cabled back on itself **13** or with a fine yarn. If you decide to use a commercial yarn in the cable, add extra twist to it before you cable.

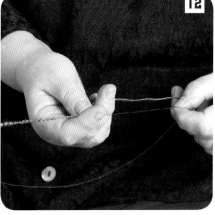
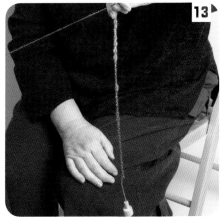
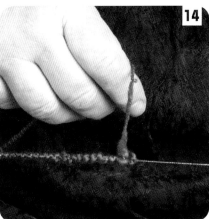

Double-Bound Silk Bouclé

Spin a bobbin of slub high-twist silk singles and use it to make a bobbin of spiraled slub yarn (see page 94). Instead of cabling the spiral slub yarn, twist it with a fine 60/2 thread in the same direction (left) and make a bouclé, entering the spiral slub yarn under less tension at a 90-degree angle to the thread. **14** (60/2 should be a staple in every spinner's closet, especially for novelty yarns. The least expensive way to buy it is on cones, in white, and dye it yourself.) Next, balance out the extreme left twist, either by cabling two of these yarns together **15** or by binding

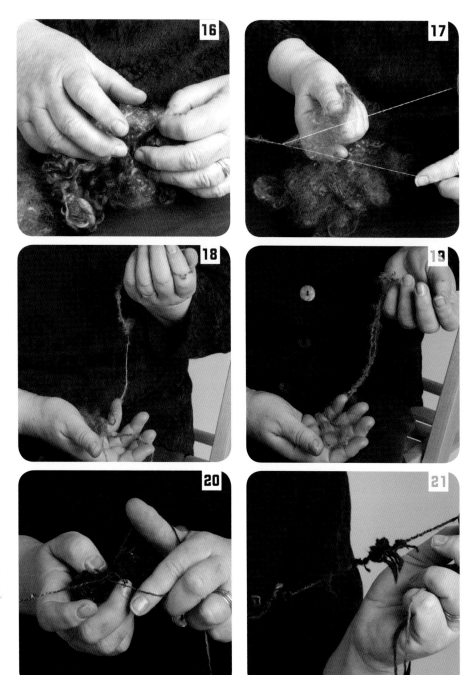

it with the same fine metallic thread held at 45 degrees, like a sloppy ply.

ENCASEMENT YARNS

Encasements are yarns that are created when two yarns are plied or cabled together with an unspun element caught in between—again, something that's easy enough to do accidentally. The high ply twist necessary to make a cable plus the extra layer of twist make these yarns suprisingly durable. It's one of a very few ancient novelty techniques. Encasement yarns have been found that are more than 5,000 years old. Encasement was also a universal technique; examples have been found in many countries. I learned to spin these yarns as a child from the Coast Salish spinners where I grew up in British Columbia, Canada. The spinners made wonderful yarns by encasing fireweed silk and eagle down between two plied cedar-bark threads.

Silk and Mohair Gossamer

This yarn uses two fine (60/2) silk threads to trap kid mohair and make a wonderful weaving yarn (warp, weft, or both) or a knitting yarn for gossamer-light garments. Set up two bobbins of firmly spun very fine two-ply as if to ply. Take a handful of dyed mohair locks and gently tease them apart; **16** some lock structure should remain in the fiber. Attach the silk threads to the bobbin, turning the wheel to tighten the ply twist of the threads. Hold the threads apart, as if you were plying. Place the mohair between the two threads just as the ply twist touches the yarn. **17** The trick is to remember to hold the fiber in the hand the yarn is rotating toward, so that it can pick up the fiber. If you hold the mohair in the hand the yarns are rotating away from, it tends to be pushed away rather than picked up. The amount of mohair you use is simply a design choice. The yarn will work well either completely covered or with the tiniest amount of fiber between. **18 19**

The silk threads have an extremely high twist, which keeps the mohair locked in place. This yarn needs to be cabled to be stable. It's a lovely soft yarn cabled back on itself, but you could also cable it with a beaded yarn, a slub yarn, or a very fine wool or silk.

With the exception of silk or cashmere and other fine, short fibers, almost any fiber will work. Try alpaca or angora. Encasement is a great technique to stretch a precious fiber like vicuña and get its maximum effect.

Recycled Treasures

This yarn encases fragments that have already been spun, woven, or knitted: fabric, thrums, bits of yarn, ribbon, silk waste, or anything else that was processed in some way from fiber. Cut the material to be encased to an appropriate length for your yarn design. Here, I've used loom waste from Pendleton wool blankets. Set up the two encasing threads. You can use any threads in any combination. Consider adding even more texture by using a fine wool or silk bouclé. Encase the fabric and yarn fragments using the same technique as for the mohair locks, **20 21** paying attention to the direction of the twist.

Feathered Yarns

Feathered yarns have been used since ancient times for decoration and ceremony. Feathers can be encased by placing them by hand between the threads as they spin

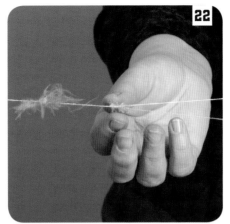

together. Parrot, ostrich, budgie, or dyed feathers from a craft supply store look wonderful spun with mohair or silk. You can use them alone or in combination with singles to make highly unusual yarns that are remarkably durable. I prefer to strip the feathers from the quill for softness. Place the feathers between the two yarns at intervals. **22** Then cable two or three of these yarns together. **23**

Beaded Yarns

To make a fairly secure beaded yarn, string the beads onto a cone or bobbin of 60/2 silk. If possible, place the cone so that it's at the same height as the orifice on your wheel to make it easier to slide the beads. Set up your wheel for encasement, attaching the encasement yarns and the beaded silk thread. As you spin, periodically slide the beads forward and place the silk and beads between the encasement threads. **24** This yarn will need to be cabled, either back on itself **25** or with a different yarn. Encasing the beads and cabling the yarn holds the beads in place more firmly than if they were simply threaded on a plying yarn.

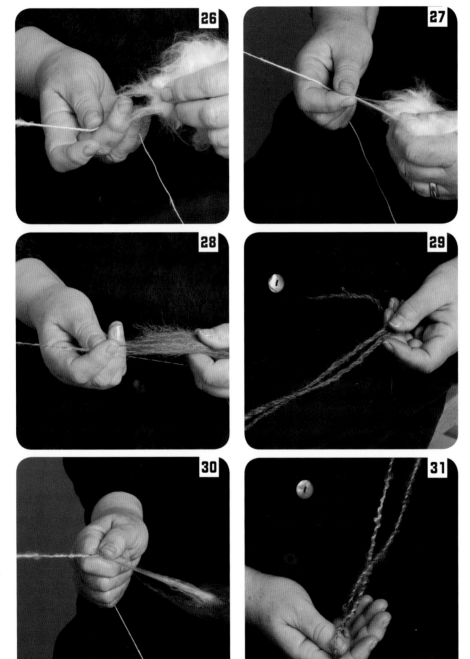

UNSPUN DESIGNS: SPINNING FIBER WITH PLIED YARN

This group of yarns is based on adding an unspun or underspun element to an already spun yarn. It magically extends the amount of precious fiber you have, as none of it is spun for the actual structure of the yarn.

Frosting

Use this technique to add fiber to an already spun yarn; it creates a beautiful halo around the yarn, softens its surface, and increases its diameter with little additional weight. Any long, straight fiber except silk will work beautifully with this method, including long fiber tops. If you have only a little of a precious fiber, frosting is another good way to stretch it out.

For this yarn, I've used a bobbin of tightly spun fine Merino spun right and angora fiber. Loosen the angora and hold it in your left hand **26** (to match the way the singles will rotate). Put the singles on a kate, attach it to your leader, and turn the wheel left as if to ply. Hold the loose fiber at right angles to the untwisting single. The fibers will catch in as the single rotates and loosens. **27** Remember that the wheel is unspinning the single as you add the fiber; if you take too long adding the fiber, all the twist will run out of the singles and the yarn will come apart as you spin. You can put as much or as little fiber on the singles as you wish. This yarn is technically still a single; you can use it as a single, ply it, or use it as part of a novelty technique.

Supported Draft

In this method, a nearly invisible strong thread is drafted with unspun fiber to make a stable yarn with a soft surface. Hold the fiber and the supporting thread in your fiber hand and pull them into the drafting zone together. **28** This yarn will need to be plied. **29**

Core Spinning

The core spinning technique is much like the frosted technique I used for the angora, except it uses a commercially spun plied yarn. The core yarn is spun back in the same direction it was plied; as the ply twist tightens, the fiber you're adding catches in the core yarn fibers. **30** The main difference between frosting and core spinning is that the core yarn is plied, and you'll need to cable it to make it stable. **31**

Twinkle Toes

I like to use this technique to add a bit of sparkle to a sock yarn. Most metallic fibers are single metallized fine plastic strips, which are not strong on their own. By supporting the metallics with a fine silk or sewing thread—just treat them as if they were one, holding them together. The fine thread will take the tension off the metallic, and the yarn will wear better, even in socks. **32**

I've used a painted Merino/silk top and drafted multicolored sewing thread and a metallic fiber with it. I've used one single of the metallic blend with two painted merino singles to make a sparkly but long-wearing sock yarn. The plying brings out the sparkle, which will appear randomly. **33**

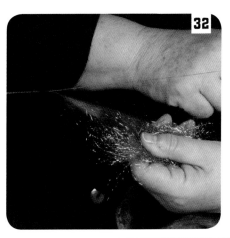

[CHAPTER SEVEN]

yarn design

WHAT IS IT THAT sparks the creative process, inspiring us to make a beautiful textile piece? For me it is often the fiber itself; I want my finished work to reveal that special quality that attracted me to the fiber in the first place. For many designers, the final piece is the key. They have a finished design in mind and work their way back to the yarn necessary to create it. Neither starting point—nor the infinite variations between them—is ultimately more successful than the other. All approaches lead back to the creation of the perfect thread.

What makes a thread perfect is simple. It's not the size or the evenness or the amount of twist or the spinning method; a perfect thread is one that will do what you want it to do. It contains the seeds of your project. The durability, the shape retention, the hand, and the surface design are carried in the thread you've spun.

Planning the Perfect Yarn

The qualities necessary in a thread vary from project to project. Yarn that will make a perfect rug and yarn for a great pair of socks are light years apart. One yarn needs to be smooth, still, and strong; the other needs to be elastic and alive with twist memory. To select qualities you can expect from a finished yarn, you need to understand the primary forces that create a yarn in the first place. Although many factors are involved in yarn design (such as texture and color), the basic qualities that make yarn work are elasticity, twist, and diameter. Elasticity and diameter both start with the fiber, even before the first singles are spun, and they're magnified or diminished through the mechanics of spinning. If you understand how all three elements work, you're well on your way to that perfect thread.

Yarn is always transformed in our hands. Our job as yarn and fabric designers is to understand how this happens and how to use it to our benefit and our great pleasure. One of the first principles of textiles is that all fiber will try to return to its original state. If you stretch and twist it, as in the spinning process, the fiber will always move toward relaxing and straightening. Spinners use that movement to create fabric. For instance, a balanced yarn is the result of two layers of twist that go in opposite directions; these opposing tensions hold the yarn still.

Elasticity

Elasticity is the ability of a fiber or a yarn to stretch and return to its original shape. Elasticity in the yarn gives a garment its ability to wear well and keep its shape. You can measure elasticity simply by stretching the fiber or yarn against a ruler, then letting it relax. Doing so helps you determine the degree of elasticity your yarn will have. The characteristic that gives fiber its elasticity is its crimp structure. Depending on the type of crimp and the amount, fibers range from no elasticity (flax, ramie, and hemp) to super elastic (nylons and wools).

The amount of elasticity that you need in a yarn depends on the project. A rug and a traditional coverlet need to stay in one place; for both of these yarns, the less elasticity the better. A good fiber choice for a rug warp is plied-worsted wet-spun flax, a fiber with no memory. The perfect coverlet warp is medium wool, firmly spun worsted and firmly plied, with its memory suppressed by the combing and spinning. The coverlet won't creep across the bed and will show the woven pattern clearly. Although socks are also spun worsted for longevity, they'll be most comfortable if they're spun from elastic fiber such as Polwarth or Merino wool. The elasticity will give the sock good memory and make it fit perfectly.

Twist

Twist is the magic glue that holds fibers together and transforms them into textiles. Sarah Natani, the remarkable Navajo weaver, tells her students that a spinner is "just like Spider Woman. Everything She touches changes and She touches everything." Using yarn always transforms it from one state to another; the twist never remains unchanged.

As a weaver, I've learned that the direction of ply twist affects the cloth you produce. To make clothing, yardage, and blankets, I use the same twist direction in both the warp and weft yarns. This lets them lock together, forming a strong but lightweight fabric. For rugs and upholstery, I use alternate twists in the warp and weft.

It doesn't appear to matter which is spun left or spun right. The different twist directions let the weft yarn move smoothly over the warp, producing a dense, smooth surface that's long-wearing, repels stains, and is lustrous. The basic principle in spinning for weaving is that the singles is always spun to the right, unless you have a good reason not to. Depending on the style of loom and whether the warp beam rolls toward or away from the loom, the twist in the yarn increases or decreases as it is wound on.

In knitting, it's a little more complicated. Knitting is a mono-element construction, a single thread looped back on itself, unlike a weaving structure whose many threads interlock at right angles. How knitters' hands move to make the stitches also affects the twist in the yarn. If you knit in the Continental style (carrying the working yarn in your left hand), you tighten the commonly used left-ply twist. If you knit as I do and as my British grandmother did (carrying the working yarn in the right hand), you relax the left-ply twist when you make your stitches.

Test these differences by knitting a sample swatch with a fairly thick yarn so you can watch the movement of the twist in the yarn. Knit Continental for six rows, then switch to English. Closely examine the stitch structure. You'll notice a change in the size of the stitches as you move from one method to the other. As a spinner, you can create a yarn that does what you want when you knit it; simply adjust your spinning direction. For knitting, the weaving convention of always spinning to the right and plying to the left doesn't apply. Spin in the direction that most enhances your knitting style.

Remember Spider Woman and pay close attention to how the yarn reacts to being handled. All the tools you use—bobbin winders, looms, ball winders or nøstepinnes, knitting needles or crochet hooks—add or remove twist as you use them.

Left, right, Z, S, clockwise, counterclockwise, widdershins, toward the sun, against the sun: all are terms that describe which way a yarn is twisted. I prefer to use the words "left" and "right" to describe the twist direction. This makes sense for a spinner because the direction that the wheel or spindle turns determines the type of twist in the yarn—turn the wheel to the right and you create a right-twist yarn, to the left, a left-twist yarn. No matter how you describe the direction of twist, you need to know what it is and how it affects the creation of cloth. Depending on your goals and how you intend to work up the yarn, you may want to choose different twist directions. For example, if you know your twist will tighten when you knit, you might choose to ply more loosely or spin in the opposite direction to counteract that tendency in your finished object.

The second principle of textiles is that twist increases the strength of multiple fibers exponentially. The more fibers twisted, the stronger the yarn; the more layers of twist, as in a plied or cabled yarn, the stronger the yarn. A well-designed yarn has just the right amount of twist: too little makes it weak and unable to withstand abrasion; too much gives it a harsh hand and might make it brittle.

Check the angle of twist in both singles and plies. I use a 45-degree angle for all my spinning unless I have a good reason not to. For example, a yarn to make a cut-pile weft would have a low twist in both the singles and the ply, letting the yarn fan out when cut and form a thick pile. Singles to make a cabled yarn would have a low twist and be plied with a high unbalanced twist, in order to be balanced when cabled. All my other yarns have a 45-degree twist, no matter the diameter or the twist per inch. The twist per inch will increase automatically as the yarn diameter decreases and decrease as the yarn diameter increases. Twist angle is determined primarily by adjusting the tension on the drive band, either by changing the pulley or tightening the drive-band tension. Increased tension will create a low-twist yarn; decreased tension will create a high-twist yarn.

You can also use the brake on a single-drive wheel to fine-tune the angle of twist; on a double-drive wheel, when you tighten one, you tighten both the bobbin and drive-wheel band.

Diameter

Two factors are largely responsible for the diameter of the yarn that you spin: the type of fiber you're spinning and the tension (or drafting-in speed) on your wheel. The right yarn diameter is, of course, the diameter that suits your current project. Nevertheless, with all the reverence for saris, burial cloth, and wedding-ring shawls, spinning fine thread is often thought of as the benchmark of a good spinner. As a young spinner, I certainly thought it was. Sometime in the early 1960s, I set myself a goal; I would spin a thread that could be used in the bobbin of my old treadle sewing machine.

At that time, I was making my living creating handspun handwoven jackets best described as conspicuously handspun—a great deal of chunky, textured yarn. I worked away, adjusting myself and the wheel, and sure enough, I was able to make a good, serviceable wool sewing thread. I also discovered that there is indeed a Goddess of Spinning Karma who keeps spinners humble. When I went to spin my plump bread-and-butter yarn for my next order, I couldn't do it. I could only spin sewing thread. I learned that spinning the yarn you need, no matter what diameter or twist per inch, is what makes a good spinner.

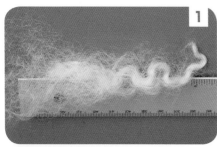

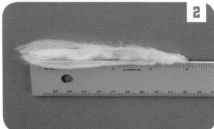

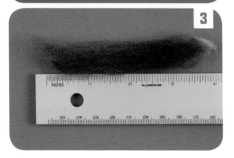

Choosing Fiber

When you choose fiber for a project, take a good look at micron, length, and crimp. Each is a key factor in the yarn you'll be able to spin.

MICRON

The micron count, or the diameter of the fiber you're spinning, plays an important role in determining the size of yarn that you can spin (see page 58). To spin a fine, consistent yarn with a good hand, the micron must be fine as well. Putting together fewer coarse fibers to make finer yarn can't produce a yarn that will have a good hand or be smooth and strong. Choosing the correct micron is an important step in designing the best yarn for the project you have in mind. For instance, you might buy 16-micron cashmere to spin an extremely fine lace yarn but 21-micron cashmere for a thicker sweater-weight yarn.

LENGTH

The length of fibers determines how you can process them. For the best carded preparation—on handcards, a drumcarder, or commercial equipment—the fibers should be 2½ inches (6.5 centimeters) or shorter. (If necessary, try cutting overlong fibers before carding.)

To comb fiber successfully, however, you need to choose fiber that is 2½ inches (6.5 centimeters) to fit on the combs properly. The fiber also needs to be strong enough to withstand the combing process, whether it's done by hand or by machine.

The length of the fiber also determines which spinning method will be the most successful. The traditional rule of thumb is that any fiber 3 inches (7.5 centimeters) or longer with fewer than 7 crimps per inch is spun with a worsted method, while any fiber 2 inches (5 centimeters) or shorter with more than 7 crimps per inch is spun in a woolen style.

CRIMP

Examine crimp carefully because it can be deceiving. Fleeces in which the crimp seems obvious often have a much lower crimp count than appears at first glance. Crimp comes in three basic styles:

- Sideways or open, a big lazy S shape found in Lincoln, Teeswater, and other luster longwools. **1**
- Front to back, a fine sawtooth edge found in Merino, Cormo, and other fine wools. **2**
- Spiral or robust, which is sideways, front to back, and twisted in a spiral; it's found in down breeds such as Suffolk, Dorset, and Hampshire. **3**

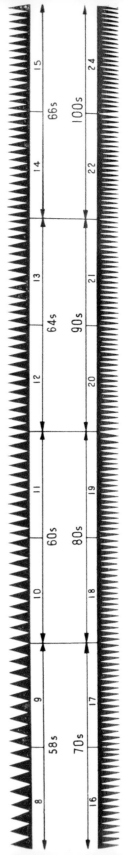

crimp meter

In fine wools, there's an interesting and well-established relationship between crimp and micron: the more crimps per inch, the finer the fiber (see the crimp meter at left). Crimp can be measured in a lab or at home using a ruler. Use a low-power magnifying lens to help you accurately see the crimp.

If the fiber has been commercially processed into top, wash a sample in hot water and let it dry before you examine it. The commercial top-making process stretches and heat-sets the fiber to suppress its natural crimp structure during spinning. After the yarn is spun, washing the skeins in hot water restores the crimp to its original shape.

Generally, if there's a lot of crimp in the fleece (especially of the robust type), you can use fewer twists per inch and achieve the same strength as you would with a fiber containing less crimp and spun with more twist. The larger the diameter of singles you want to produce, the more crimp the fiber should have. For example, if you want to spin yarn to knit a Cowichan sweater, you would choose a fleece with a robust crimp, such as North Country Cheviot, Dorset, or a down-breed cross. Even knitted from a bulky, low-twist single, the sweater would hold its shape. It would be lightweight, warm, and long-lasting. If the same size singles were made with Romney or Lincoln, both luster longwools with classic S-shaped crimp, the sweater would stretch and bag, unable to hold its shape. The sweater would also be much too heavy to wear comfortably. Combed and spun into a fine three-ply, that same Romney fleece would make an incredible Aran cable sweater that would hold its shape and wear for generations.

For different types of yarn, these guidelines might be put aside. One example is "wet" spun Merino and silk. A Merino or Merino-silk blend top can be spun in a lofty Lopi-style yarn and be quite stable if it's finished correctly. Put it in hot soapy water and agitate it (see pages 110–111). The fibers will felt slightly, locking the yarn together. The slight felting will create the stability that neither the fiber nor the yarn structure has, letting this yarn make an interesting surface and texture in knitted or woven fabric.

Once you've chosen the fleece for your project and taken its structure into consideration, the next thing to consider is yarn diameter. Determine the diameter by the yarn's function. For instance, Corriedale top might be spun into three-ply sportweight yarn because it has enough crimp to make a great yarn for a warm, lightweight sweater. It could also be spun into a fine two-ply for a lace scarf, because it's long enough to be combed and spun worsted, and it lacks an extreme crimp structure that could distort the lace pattern.

In addition, you could use it to spin a fine warp yarn for a blanket; it has enough crimp to make a wonderfully warm lightweight yarn, and it's long and strong enough to be combed, which would help make it a better warp. Carded and spun semiwoolen for a weft yarn, Corriedale would full a bit and lock the warp and weft together to make a durable fabric. In other words, you can choose to prepare and spin this fiber in various ways, and the combination of preparation, drafting technique, and diameter you choose will determine how you can use the yarn.

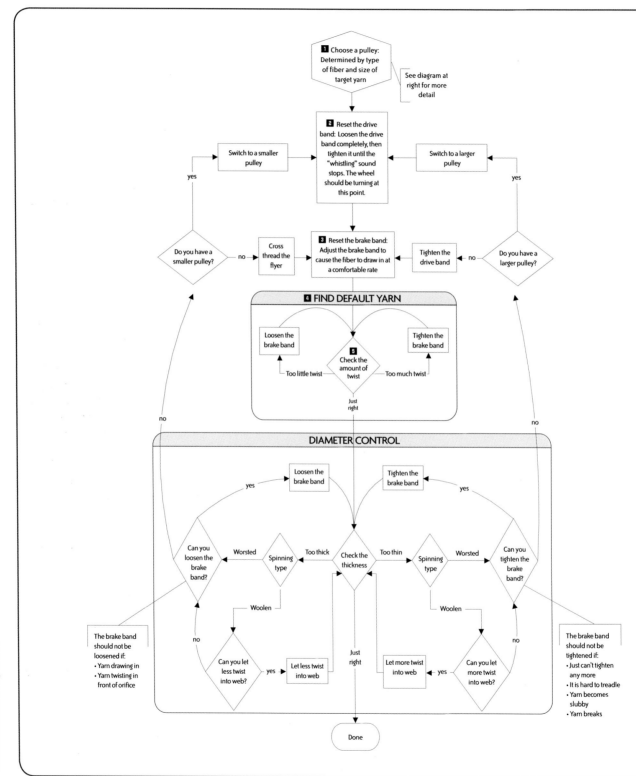

1 Choose a pulley: Determined by type of fiber and size of target yarn

See diagram at right for more detail

2 Reset the drive band: Loosen the drive band completely, then tighten it until the "whistling" sound stops. The wheel should be turning at this point.

Switch to a smaller pulley

Switch to a larger pulley

yes

yes

Do you have a smaller pulley?

no

Cross thread the flyer

3 Reset the brake band: Adjust the brake band to cause the fiber to draw in at a comfortable rate

Tighten the drive band

no

Do you have a larger pulley?

4 FIND DEFAULT YARN

Loosen the brake band

Tighten the brake band

5 Check the amount of twist

Too little twist

Too much twist

Just right

DIAMETER CONTROL

Loosen the brake band

Tighten the brake band

yes

yes

Can you loosen the brake band?

Worsted

Spinning type

Too thick

Check the thickness

Too thin

Spinning type

Worsted

Can you tighten the brake band?

Woolen

Woolen

no

no

The brake band should not be loosened if:
• Yarn drawing in
• Yarn twisting in front of orifice

Can you let less twist into web?

yes

Let less twist into web

Just right

Let more twist into web

yes

Can you let more twist into web?

The brake band should not be tightened if:
• Just can't tighten any more
• It is hard to treadle
• Yarn becomes slubby
• Yarn breaks

Done

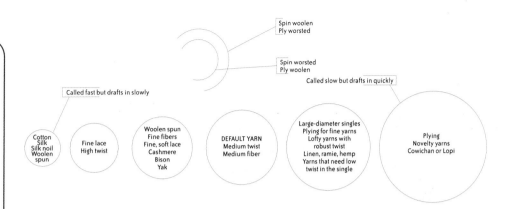

Spin woolen
Ply worsted

Spin worsted
Ply woolen

Called slow but drafts in quickly

Called fast but drafts in slowly

| Cotton Silk Silk noil Woolen spun | Fine lace High twist | Woolen spun Fine fibers Fine, soft lace Cashmere Bison Yak | DEFAULT YARN Medium twist Medium fiber | Large-diameter singles Plying for fine yarns Lofty yarns with robust twist Linen, ramie, hemp Yarns that need low twist in the single | Plying Novelty yarns Cowichan or Lopi |

HOW TO USE THE SPINNING FLOWCHART

To adjust the diameter of your yarn, it is much simpler and more effective to adjust the wheel than to change your natural rhythm.

1 Choose a pulley, referring to the chart at right.

2 Starting with the drive band very slack, slowly tighten the drive band until you can no longer hear the band slipping over the wheel and the pulley is turning.

3 Starting with the brake band completely slack, slowly tighten the tension until the flyer takes up the yarn at a comfortable rate—for worsted, when you can easily keep the twist out of the drafting zone; for woolen, when the twist runs into the drafting zone but not into the fiber supply. Do the same if you are using a double-drive wheel—but you will be adjusting both bands at the same time.

4 Spin at a relaxed rate, allowing the yarn to spin at the grist your natural rhythm creates.

5 Use the plyback test to determine if the twists per inch or twist angle is what you want and adjust as needed.

Continue making adjustments as given on the chart until you are making the desired yarn, changing the pullry if necessary.

Remember, you should match the drafting-in speed of the wheel to the natural rhythm of your hands. The right pulley and tension will do the rest.

Diameter Control

When I was a beginning spinner, I was delighted to simply produce a continuous thread. I couldn't have told anyone what spinning method I was using, and truly I wasn't interested. I just wanted to make yarn and was happy to spin whatever the wheel would let me have. It wasn't long before I had the same complaint that I hear from many intermediate spinners—they can't spin anything but fine.

This quandary has more to do with how you spin than what you spin with. When you spin, you use both your hands and your feet in an unsyncopated rhythm, like waltzing with your hands and marching with your toes. That means the information is stored in an old, primitive part of your brain, the part Carl Sagan called the "crocodile brain." Just like the crocodile, whatever this part of your brain grabs onto, it holds onto forever. That's usually a good thing because this part of your brain controls important functions like breathing and heartbeat. However, it also holds onto your spinning rhythm. And when you try to change—speed up or slow down your hands or your feet to change the type of yarn you're spinning—the automatic

rhythm returns the minute you stop paying close attention, giving you the same diameter time after time.

The trick to controlling the yarn's diameter is to use this automatic rhythm to your advantage: learn to adjust the wheel instead of your body. Remember that you and the wheel are partners; spinning is like playing a violin. The wheel, your instrument, becomes an extension of your physical self. Spinning-wheel designers have given you many ways to adjust the wheel; you can change the speed at which the yarn feeds on and the twist per inch. By changing your hands minimally (and without changing the speed of your feet), you can use these adjustments to change the diameter of the yarn.

When you're adjusting your wheel tension, think of your wheel as a musical instrument, not as a chain saw. Make adjustments in tiny increments, preferably with the wheel in motion. Look for the place where the yarn flows off your fingers like water over stone.

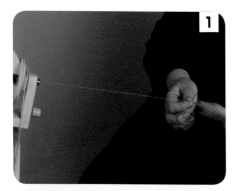
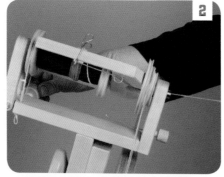
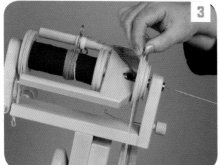
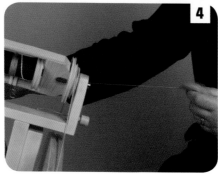
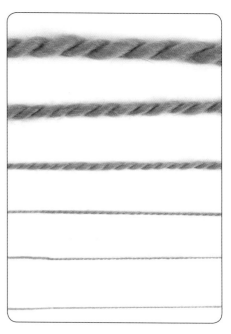

Without changing hand or foot speed, I made this wide range of two-ply yarns with small adjustments to the wheel.

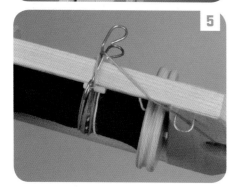

WORSTED DIAMETER

To explore the diameter changes that your wheel can help you achieve, first find the normal weight of yarn you spin when you're not thinking about a specific yarn. This weight is your "default" yarn. **1** Without changing your treadling, gently increase the tension on the wheel. **2** If you keep the pressure in your drafting hand constant, the yarn will automatically thicken as the increased draw pulls more fiber into the drafting zone. (Be careful not to tighten your hand as you feel the drafting tension increase.)

The stronger the take-up, the thicker the yarn will be. If the wheel becomes difficult to treadle when you're aiming for a thicker yarn, it's time to move up a pulley size. **3** If you don't have a choice of pulley sizes, add a little more tension to the drive band. A rough correlation to diameter in worsted is pulley size: the larger the pulley, the larger the yarn.

To spin a finer yarn than you usually do, simply take a little tension off the wheel. Again, be careful not to adjust your treadling or your drafting speed. When the tension on the wheel is reduced, less fiber is drawn into the drafting zone. You can then draw the yarn out finer because the yarn is pulled onto the bobbin more slowly.

Keep decreasing the tension until you get the diameter you want effortlessly, no matter what diameter you're spinning. If you reach a point at which you cannot decrease the diameter of the yarn any more without it pulling out of your hands, move to a smaller pulley or reduce the tension on your drive band. **4** When you've reached the limit to this adjustment, the drive band will start slipping. To spin even finer yarn, cross-lace the yarn using hooks on both sides of the flyer. **5** Every hook used for this purpose is the equivalent decreasing of a pulley size. You can cross-lace other types of flyers by looping the yarn behind the sliding hook or behind the arm of the WooLee Winder.

WOOLEN DIAMETER

In woolen spinning, diameter control follows a similar principle—with a slight twist! Instead of increasing or decreasing the tension, let more or less twist into the web. The more twist you let into the web without starting to draw back, the thicker the yarn will be; the less twist you let enter the web, the finer the yarn will be. It can be difficult, especially for people who are more comfortable spinning worsted, to let enough twist build up to maintain the diameter of the yarn. One trick is to treadle three or four times with your fingers keeping the twist out of the web, then release it before you start to draw back. Continue to release enough twist to maintain the yarn's diameter as you continue drawing back, more to thicken it, less to thin it.

The Importance of Plying

Plying is one of the surest ways to create a consistent yarn (see page 82–84). Ply unless you have a good reason not to. (There are good reasons, as in Kathryn Alexander's work, where the amazing textures and patterns depend on the wild twist energy of the singles.) By releasing a bit of the twist energy, plying lets the twist run smoothly through the yarn and redistribute itself more evenly throughout its entire length. It gives another opportunity to correct thick and thin places and to place an evenly measured final twist on the yarn. Remember that consistency doesn't

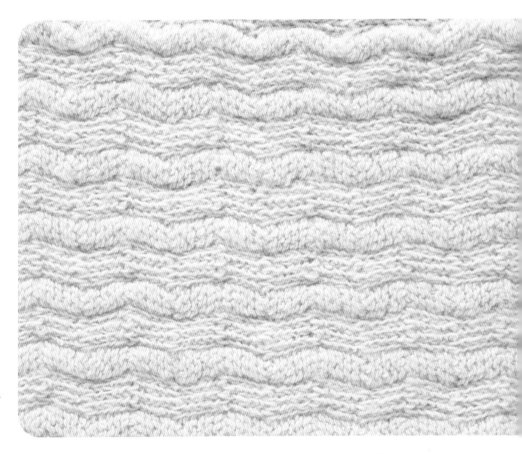

mean that it's necessarily an even surfaced yarn—it means that inconsistencies are evenly distributed throughout the skeins in a project. A yarn can be consistent even if the number of plies varies throughout the yarn.

Designing your yarn includes deciding on a plying structure, which affects the diameter of the singles you spin in the first place. The increase effect in diameter decreases as the number of plies rises: there is a big difference between a single, a two-ply, and a three-ply, less difference between a four-ply, five-ply, and six-ply.

The movement in this fabric by textile artist Kathryn Alexander is created using reverse-twist energized singles. These singles transform a simple rib into an elaborate zigzag pattern.

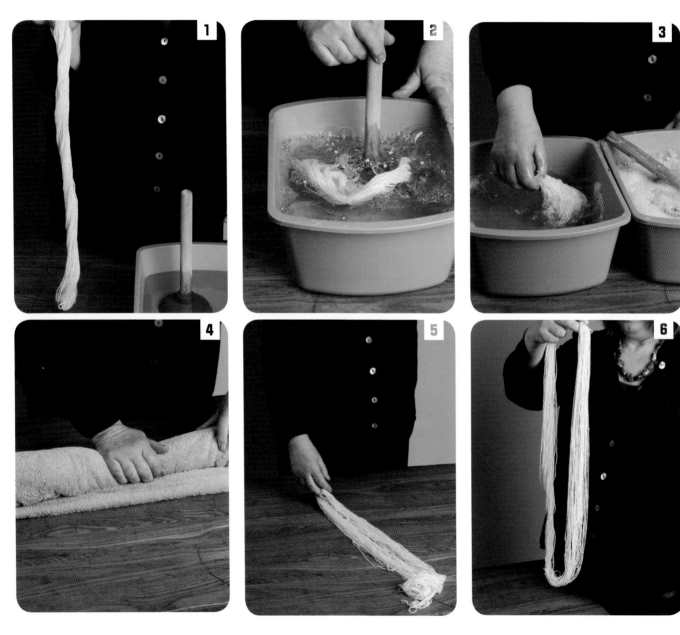

Finishing

Your yarn isn't finished when it's wound off on a niddy-noddy; you could even say it isn't finished until it has been transformed into its final form. Washing your yarn is often an important step toward working with it. Don't worry if a skein of yarn twists when it's wound right off the bobbin; **1** a hot bath will transform it. Finishing yarn helps distribute the twist evenly and removes any spinning oil. When you sample for yarn design, finish a small skein as you plan to finish the final yarn.

You may not want to finish the yarn in the skein if you plan to alter the fabric through finishing. For a woven and fulled scarf (see page 130) or a knitted and fulled bag, you'll probably want to finish the piece rather than the yarn. Traditionally, weaving yarns are used unfinished, both warp and weft, allowing the finishing of the yarns to create the stability of the fabric.

For most worsted yarns, cellulose fibers, and silk, soak the yarn in hot water with a little wool wash, press out as much of the water as possible, then soak it in tepid water to rinse out the soap. After pressing out the water, let it hang unweighted to dry.

For many woolen yarns, especially those made with short keratin fibers, a more aggressive fulling wash will make the yarn stronger and more stable as well as enhance the surface texture.

Fill one basin with very hot water and add detergent; fill another with cold water.

Place the yarn in the hot water and agitate it; I like to use a sink plunger for this process. **2** Squeeze out the hot, soapy water and plunge the skein in the cold water. Swish it around in the cold water, then wring it out and return it to the hot, soapy water for more agitation. **3**

Repeat this process three or four times; you'll know the yarn is ready when it begins to soften up and bloom. Stop after a cool rinse. Remove the skein from the water, wrap it in a towel, and squeeze the water out. **4** Snap the skein firmly against a table or counter several times. **5** The yarn should be softer and more cohesive, and the skein will be much more relaxed. **6** (For a more detailed explanation of finishing, see "Wet Finishes for Yarn," *Spin·Off*, Summer 2007.)

Sample, Sample, Sample

Don't think for a moment that sampling is a waste of time and yarn. Nothing is more disheartening than to go through the fiber preparation, the spinning, and the construction of the fabric, only to find that your vision of the cloth has vanished somewhere along the way. There is simply no substitute for sampling; try to think of it as an interesting practice.

Do your first sample before you have everything spun up; it will be much easier to fix anything that you don't like at this point than after you have spun and plied it all (although most matters can usually be corrected even after yarn is plied). I spin

half a bobbin at the most before I make a few small sample skeins. Try a few different plies, if that's appropriate. Finish these skeins as you would the whole project. Check to make sure you have enough twist to make the yarn you want when you ply it or for the yarn to behave as desired if you use it as a single.

If I'm experimenting with a new yarn and want to know how it will hold up, I knit a pair of cuffs and wear them for a couple of weeks. If I'm still happy with them, I can be fairly confident that the yarn will wear well either knitted or woven into a garment.

If I need to spin for a specific yardage, I check the yardage of my sample using a McMorran balance (see page 59). If I need a specific diameter, especially for a knitting yarn, I use either a millimeter measuring tape or my needle gauge. (If you're looking for the right needle size to make a gauge swatch for a knitting project, fold the yarn in half and see which hole it slips into perfectly. Start sampling with that size needle. Go up a needle size and down a needle size and compare the resulting swatches.)

One way to understand what makes a successful yarn is to take a good look at fabrics and garments that have stood the test of time. Check the amount of twist, the number of plies, and the type of fiber if you can. Keep samples of commercial yarns that you have enjoyed working with and analyze their structure. Build a "library" of yarn characteristics.

CHAPTER EIGHT

four intermediate spinning projects

The painter Johannes Itten has been a major influence in my work. While Itten was not a textile artist, I have benefited from his understanding of design and color principles. I also learned from him that theory is always extracted from practical experience. To paraphrase Itten, if you want to go on a long journey, use a vehicle, but to take an interesting journey, you need to get out and walk. Theory is the vehicle to take you to the start of that interesting journey.

Each of these four projects is designed to reinforce spinning theories with practical experience, taking you through the steps from fiber to fabric. (They don't include basic knitting or weaving definitions. Consult a guidebook such as *The Knitter's Companion* and *The Weaver's Companion* to help with basic information.)

Spinning Fine Yarn for Lace

When I've traveled to countries where handspinning is part of the everyday work world, I'm often amazed at the fine, perfect yarns the people spin. Sometimes I'm a little envious—they never have to hear "Why would you spin that? Couldn't a machine do it?" In many cultures, spinning a fine yarn shows mastery of your craft. Although it's not the only criterion for a handspinner in the industrial world, it's satisfying to spin a perfect, simple thread. It still feels like spinning magic to me.

CHOOSING FIBER

To spin a fine yarn, the first thing you need is fine fiber. You can always draft out a fine micron fiber, whether animal, vegetable, or synthetic, more easily and evenly than coarse fiber. Choose fiber that's 22 microns or finer to produce a fine yarn with a good hand.

For this lace yarn, I used a commercial blend of depigmented yak and Merino. I've been smitten with this blend from the first time my hands touched it; it's pure pleasure to spin. Even though I knew that the downy fiber wouldn't produce the clearest pattern definition, I also knew that its fine micron count (17 microns for the yak and 21 microns for the Merino) and its incredible hand would make the scarf feel lovely against bare skin. Its fineness also makes it easy to spin a consistent laceweight yarn. I spun 2 ounces (57 grams) into about 270 yards (247 meters) of finished two-ply yarn for this wonderfully wearable little scarf, designed and knitted by Ruth Hollowell.

Many other fibers would be suitable:

cashmere or a silk/cashmere blend would be perfect, as would pure silk, any Merino/cashmere blend, bison, yak, angora, camel, or baby alpaca, just to name a few possibilities. The stitch definition will depend on the fiber and whether you use a true worsted or semiwoolen draw. However, all these fibers will have an exquisite hand.

SPINNING METHOD

You can spin fine yarns on any wheel; it's a matter of adjustment. If you run out of ways to adjust the wheel, then you can adjust yourself. If possible, choose a scotch-brake system, which gives the most control for fine spinning. Avoid a bobbin-driven or irish-tension wheel if possible because it will mean a great deal more adjustment on your part.

Lace yarns require a slow draw-in speed and relatively high twist per inch (see pages 108–109). Once your wheel is adjusted, make sure that your hands are relaxed and the fiber can move into the drafting zone easily. Check that you're drafting out the correct amount of fiber for the diameter you want: if you draft out too much, the yarn will become larger than you intended; if you draft out too little, the diameter will be too small.

I've spun this yarn semiwoolen, letting

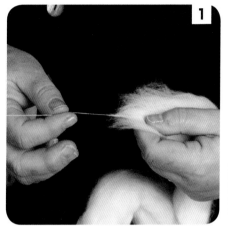
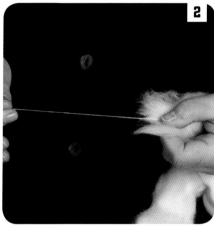

a little twist go into the web, **1** then drafting toward the wheel **2** to bring the fibers more into alignment (though not as aligned as in a worsted-spun yarn). This approach gives the down-fiber-based yarn more stability and better stitch definition than spinning it as a true woolen. I kept a firm twist on the single, knowing that it would relax quite a bit when I plied and washed it. The fiber has a silky feel, which usually means that the scale on the fiber has been flattened (or, in the case of this depigmented yak, removed). Therefore, the fiber will slip easily out of the structure of the yarn. I wanted the yarn to bloom a bit but not so much that it would completely obscure the pattern.

I spun this yarn using a scotch-brake system and a small a pulley for very minimal draw-in. You can further reduce the drafting-in speed by using a half-full bobbin, cross-lacing your wheel, or using a fat-core bobbin.

Because I'm spinning a yarn for knitting lace, I chose a two-ply yarn. Lace structure

is based on a pattern of loops, and two-ply yarn makes a crisper loop when the needle twists the yarn into a stitch. In two-ply yarn, the yarn moves away from the center of the stitch, unlike a three or more ply, which opens up into the center of the stitch. I've used a fairly firm twist for the ply.

Because the yarn has a firm ply, it will twist a bit to the right in the skein before it's washed. This slight plying overtwist will be released in the washing process. I washed the skein well in hot, soapy water, agitating it to mesh the short fibers together. Then I rinsed it in cold water to help lock the loose fibers in place (see pages 110–111). This "fulling" won't have quite the same effect on a semiwoolen yarn as it would on a woolen yarn. (Had I spun this blend with a true woolen draw, the yarn would have developed a halo and doubled in size after washing. It would have been a lightweight, amazingly soft and stable yarn, but it would have little to no stitch definition.) I dyed the yarn using low-impact synthetic dyes for wool and silk.

three-cornered scarf

by Ruth Hollowell

This scarf is lovely in a variety of yarns and gauges. Once you've made one, you'll be able to take the pattern in many directions. The size of the finished scarf can vary from small to shawl-sized.

FINISHED SIZE
Custom, based on gauge and desired size. Scarf shown measures 58" (147.5 cm) wide across top edge and 22" (56 cm) long from cast-on to bottom point.

FIBER
50% Merino/
50% depigmented yak top.

DRAFTING METHOD
Semiwoolen.

PLIED TWISTS PER INCH
28–30 tpi.

PLIED WRAPS PER INCH
27–30 wpi.

YARDS PER POUND
2,475 [2263 m].

YARDAGE USED
270 yd [248 m].

GAUGE
18 sts and 32 rows = 4" [10 cm] in garter stitch.

NEEDLE SIZE
U.S. size 7 (4.5 mm). Adjust needle size if necessary to obtain the desired gauge and fabric.

NOTIONS
2 markers (m); tapestry needle.

Scarf

Cast on 7 sts.
Set-up row: K3, place marker (pm), k1, pm, knit to end.

GARTER SECTION

Row 1: Knit into the front and back of the first st (k1f&b), knit to marker, yarnover (yo), slip marker (sl m), k1, sl m, yo, knit to last st, k1f&b—4 sts increased. (If desired, mark Row 2 to indicate which side of the scarf increases should be made on.)
Row 2: Knit.
Rep Rows 1 and 2 four more times—27 sts.

LACE SECTION

Lace row 1: K1f&b, [yo, k2tog] to m, yo, sl m, k1, sl m, yo, [k2tog, yo] to last stitch, k1f&b—4 sts increased.
Lace row 2: K1, [yo, k2tog] to m, sl m, k1, sl m, [k2tog, yo] to last stitch, k1—31 sts.
Work garter section and lace section alternately until the scarf is about two-thirds the desired size, then increase (k1f&b) on the first and last sts of every row to create "tails" on the triangle, which makes it easier

to wear. Continue until scarf measures ¼" (6 mm) less than the desired length.

EDGING

Next row: [K1, yo] to last st, k1.
Use the standard bind-off to secure all stitches. Weave in loose ends. Block as desired.

VARIATIONS

- Use stockinette stitch instead of garter stitch.

- Change the number of rows between lace panels or omit lace.

- Change the lace pattern (consult a stitch dictionary such as *The Harmony Guides: Lace & Eyelets*).

- Instead of one center stitch between yarnovers, work a lace panel at the center back and increase on both sides of it.

- Create a ruffled edge by increasing into every stitch on every other row for several rows, then binding off.

Spinning Perfect Sock Yarn

I've spent a lot of my life outdoors, usually in boots, and I have a keen appreciation for the well-designed sock! Sock yarns need to be strong, smooth, and elastic. They need to be sturdy to withstand the abrasion caused by the rubbing motion of your foot in your shoe. Few things are as disheartening as a handmade sock that doesn't wear as long as it took to spin and knit.

A yarn that can be knitted into a smooth, even surface will do more than wear well—it will also be comfortable on your foot. Feet are incredibly sensitive, and thick and thin surfaces (as well as uneven amounts of twist) will make socks uncomfortable to wear and can even raise blisters.

A sock should fit like a second skin. The more snugly a sock fits your foot, the better it withstands abrasion because it simply can't move around much. The snugness also makes a sock more comfortable to wear because there's less friction on your skin.

CHOOSING FIBER

When I'm spinning sock yarn, I look for an elastic fiber that has lots of "memory"—the inherent ability of a fiber to return to its natural state. Whenever possible, look for a fiber that has a high-crimp structure. Good crimp is the best possible way to make a yarn with good memory.

Wool top is available by breed in a wide range of natural and dyed colors. Socks benefit from using high-crimp wool.

My favorites are Polwarth, Rambouillet, Columbia, Targhee, Perendale, and Merino. Choose top and not roving, which will have too many different microns and fiber lengths to make a good sock yarn. Check to make sure that it truly is top—that all the fibers are similar in length and micron.

You can buy superwash top if you want to machine-wash your socks; any fiber that has been depigmented will be shrink-resistant as well. One drawback to machine-washable wools is that their ability to lock together mechanically is destroyed by the processing. Without scales, the wool fiber will need more twist to hold it together. Some blends of natural and shrink-resistant fiber retain the best of both worlds—the treated wool helps the blend resist shrinking, and the natural wool gives the yarn some structure.

Exotic blends such as silk and cashmere, yak and Merino, and silk and Merino would all be lovely for a special pair of socks. If you decide to use a blend, make sure the blend is fairly well mixed. If it's in chunks of different fiber, it will be difficult to draft out a smooth yarn with an even twist. Sometimes the best way to blend different fibers is to spin them separately and ply them together. A single of Merino, one of silk, and one of angora would make a wonderful three-ply sock yarn.

If I choose a fiber like silk or cotton that has little memory, I can increase the elasticity of my sock fabric by my choice of knitting structure. A rib pattern or any elastic lace or cable pattern can help give a sock more memory, which lets it wear well and hold its shape better. (If you're not sure whether a stitch pattern will be elastic, swatch!) Although strength should always be the first consideration in choosing a fleece for spinning a sock yarn, fineness in fiber counts as well. Fineness ensures that the surface of the yarn will be as smooth as possible.

SPINNING METHOD

The sock cuff can be made out of any yarn—beaded, bouclé, feathered—but the foot portion should be a good worsted yarn. Few things in the textile world are cast in concrete, but using a worsted draw for making sock yarn is one of them. Worsted yarn has all the attributes that a sock yarn needs: it's strong, smooth, and resilient. It also resists felting—a plus with socks because they'll be washed often.

No matter what diameter you choose to spin for your sock yarn, spin a firm worsted yarn. Twist is released in the plying process, and a little more is released for every ply. When you knit your swatch (I sample with yarn from my first quarter bobbin), look for a smooth, firm surface. Remember that top is directional, and make sure you're spinning it in the right direction. Try not to disturb the order of the top—avoid splitting it apart or predrafting.

Yarn for socks should be at least three-ply; a two-ply yarn won't wear as well or have as smooth a surface. It might mean spinning a bit finer, but the knitting will be a pleasure. Try four or five plies; they produce an even smoother and rounder yarn. Cables are also a good choice and a lovely way to work with color and different fibers.

Don't be overly concerned if your sock yarn seems overplied when it comes directly off the wheel. Wash it in warm, soapy water, spin the excess water out, and hang it to dry. Knit a swatch in the round. If the sock fabric is distorted and won't lie straight, try a smaller needle size. If this doesn't correct the problem, run the yarn quickly back through the wheel to the right to remove a bit of the ply twist.

MARLED SPINNING

The word "marl," from the same root as "marble," refers to a pattern of solid and swirled colors. I've chosen the marling technique to spin this sock yarn because it makes any simple pattern interesting to knit, and the yarn itself is fun to spin. Marling lets you spin like a painter, placing color where you want it, without the need to be a skilled dyer. It has the advantage of being perfectly repeatable, bobbin after bobbin, which isn't always possible with space-dyed tops. As long as you have the same colors of top in the same width, the color patterns will repeat. Natural colors are wonderful marled as well—I love the stony, striated effect of spinning natural shades.

And marled yarn is a pure pleasure to

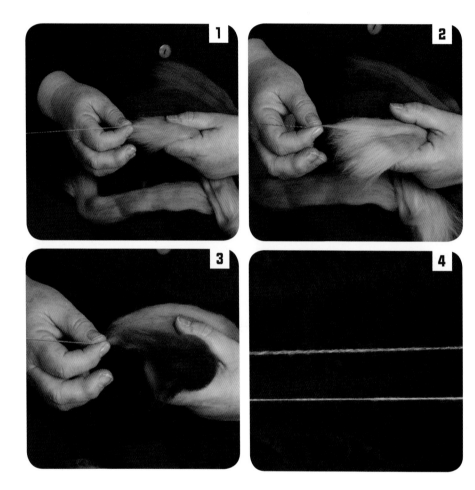

creates, though I also like marling when all the colors are close in either tone or value. You don't need to limit the number of colors you want to work with, but I wouldn't use fewer than three because the result isn't as interesting. If you aren't totally comfortable choosing colors, use a color wheel to help.

Break off a 6–8" (15–20.5 cm) length of each color. Pick up three of the colors and hold them side by side in your fiber hand. (I don't have a big hand, so three is about all I can hold flat comfortably.) Using a worsted draw, start from one side and spin across to the other, drafting the first color to start, **1** then a mix of the first and second colors, **2** then a solid of the second, a mix of the second and third colors, then a solid of the third color.

If you find that one of the colors in your hand isn't drawing out properly, try turning it around. You might be spinning it from the wrong end. Check to see which way the fibers have been combed: hold each piece 3–4" (7.5–10 cm) from one end and give the end a little tug, then tug the opposite end. Spin from the end that pulls out most easily. (You might not be able to tell which end is correct at first, but you will with practice.)

Reverse direction and spin back across from the third color to the second to the first, producing a solid, a mix, a solid, a mix, and a solid as you go. Repeat this color pattern until you're about halfway through the lengths of top. Stop, drop the last color in your spinning sequence, and add a new color in your spinning sequence. **3** Keep spinning and rotating the colors through the system you've chosen. Each time you

spin! Because commercial top is still in its pressed state (aligned, the crimp unactivated, unchanged by a trip through the dye pot), the fiber drafts effortlessly. Although the best repeatability in color sequence comes from worsted-spun marled yarns, marled yarns don't have to be spun worsted. You can spin them woolen or semiwoolen, depending on the project you have in mind.

For my socks, I've chosen fine Merino top in four colors. Corriedale or a wool/silk blend would have also made a beautiful pair of socks, but I love the fineness and the silky surface this Merino produces. This technique generally works best if all the tops are the same fiber and prepared by the same company because it will all draft out at the same speed. In any case, try to work with different fibers of similar length.

Select the colors you want to use. I've chosen to use four colors, three close in color range and one quite different, holding three at a time in my hand and rotating the fourth. I like the rich jewel-like colors this drop a color and replace it with a new one, it changes the order of the color, creating new color blends. **4**

Remember to move your yarn forward on the hooks often as you spin so the bobbin fills smoothly. You should see the color patterns form on your bobbin—marled yarns make beautiful bobbins as well as beautiful socks.

If you find it difficult to keep the fibers in order, try spinning just two colors at a time. You can even spin just one at a time, lay it down, and pick up the next until you feel confident; it doesn't create quite the same effect, but it will still be lovely. Add another color when you're ready.

When you first try this technique, you may develop a death grip on the fibers. If this happens, nothing can make the twist pull the top out of your hand, so the single will become overtwisted and thinner than you want. Try to relax your hand. Think of your hand as stones on the bottom of a river—the fiber moves like water over the stones, smoothly and effortlessly. Remember that twist is like glue; it's what holds the fiber world together. If the twist slides into the web of fibers between your hands, the twist will glue the web shut. Stop, break off the fiber, and start again.

Marling is a good way to learn to move across the top of the web while spinning worsted. If you end up with points rather than a blocky web **5** or if you struggle to direct the twist into the next color and start to spin down the side of the top, **6** you know you're letting the twist slip past your fingers into the attenuated fibers. When you have worked across all the

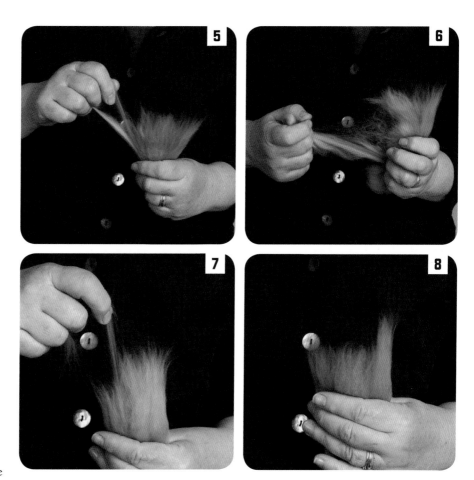

colors in your hand, the ends of the top should be even. **7** **8**

For these socks, I spun 2½ ounces (71 grams) of singles on three bobbins. I spun one bobbin of singles slightly finer than the other two because I like the color effect and slight texture this creates when knitted. For a perfectly consistent yarn, remember to rewind your bobbins before plying (see pages 83–84). Ply the three bobbins together with a firm twist; remember that you'll lose twist when you finish the skeins.

techniques | projects

perfect socks

The following pattern is based on two simple measurements; use it with any weight handspun and to fit any foot. Once you understand the basic principles behind sock construction, you can create your own patterns. (I'm usually more successful at making a pattern fit a yarn than making a yarn fit a pattern.) Be sure to try the socks on frequently and make adjustments if necessary so that they fit perfectly.

Swatch

Knit a large swatch in stockinette stitch in the round to find your gauge. Make a swatch 3–4" (7.5–10 cm) around and several inches tall to be as accurate as possible, and count fractions of stitches if necessary.

Find your ankle bone and run your finger up the bone until the bone disappears. Measure around your ankle at this point without rounding off. Multiply your ankle circumference by the number of stitches per inch. If necessary, round to an even number and increase or decrease as needed for your desired stitch pattern.

Leg

Loosely cast on the required number of stitches (make sure it's a multiple of 4) and divide as evenly as possible between three dpns.

Rnd 1: *K2, p2; rep from *.
Rnd 2: *K2tog but leave sts on left needle, knit into the front of the first st again, drop sts from left needle, p2; rep from *.
Rnds 3–4: *K2, p2; rep from *.

Repeat Rnds 1–4 for pattern until sock measures 3" (7.5 cm) or desired length to top of heel.

FINISHED SIZE
Custom, based on gauge and desired size. Socks shown here measure 7¾" (19.5 cm) ankle circumference (unstretched) and 9" (23 cm) from back of heel to tip of toe.

FIBER
100% Merino top.

DRAFTING METHOD
Worsted.

PLIED TWISTS PER INCH
15–18.

PLIED WRAPS PER INCH
18–20.

YARDS PER POUND
1,460 [1335 m].

YARDAGE USED
230 yd [210 m].

GAUGE
30 sts and 42 rnds = 4" [10 cm] in twisted rib pattern worked in the round.

NEEDLE SIZE
U.S. size 2 (2.75 mm): set of 4 or 5 double-pointed needles (dpns). Adjust needle size if necessary to obtain the desired gauge and fabric.

NOTIONS
Marker (m); tapestry needle.

TURN HEEL

Place marker (pm) at the center of the heel flap. Work short-rows to turn heel as follows:

Short-row 1: Sl 1, knit to m, sl m, k2, ssk, k1.

Short-row 2: Sl 1, purl to m, sl m, p2, purl 2 sts together (p2tog), p1.

Short-row 3: Sl 1, knit to 1 stitch before gap created on previous row, ssk (1 stitch from each side of gap), k1.

Short-row 4: Sl 1, purl to 1 stitch before gap created on previous row, p2tog (1 stitch from each side of gap), p1.

Repeat Short-rows 3 and 4 until all the stitches have been worked, ending with a knit row. (On the last two rows, omit the knit or purl stitch after the decrease if there are not enough stitches to do so.) There will be one slipped selvedge stitch on each edge of the heel flap for every two rows worked. Arrange the heel stitches as evenly as possible so that one-half of the heel stitches are on Needle 1, held instep stitches are on Needle 2, and the remaining heel stitches are on Needle 3. Knit to end of Needle 3; this will be the beginning of the round.

SHAPE GUSSETS

Set-up rnd: With Needle 1, knit the heel stitches, then pick up and knit 1 stitch in every slipped selvedge stitch along the edge of the heel flap plus 1 stitch between the

Heel

HEEL FLAP

Place half the stitches on a holder to be worked later for the instep. (To continue the pattern smoothly down the instep, I divided for the heel in the middle of a k2 pair.)

Arrange the remaining stitches on a single dpn. Work the heel back and forth in rows. Slip all stitches purlwise.

Row 1: (RS) *Slip 1 stitch (sl 1), knit 1; repeat from * to end.

Row 2: Sl 1, purl to end.

Repeat Rows 1 and 2 until the heel flap measures about 2½" (6.5 cm) or until it reaches the bottom of your heel, ending with a purl row.

heel and instep. With Needle 2, work the instep stitches, continuing the leg pattern if desired. With Needle 3, pick up and knit 1 stitch between the instep and the heel, pick up and knit 1 stitch in every slipped selvedge stitch along the edge of the heel flap, then knit to end of round.

Rnd 1: On Needle 1, knit to the last 3 sts, k2tog, k1; on Needle 2, work in the established pattern; on Needle 3, k1, ssk, knit to end of round—2 stitches decreased.

Rnd 2: On Needle 1, knit; on Needle 2, work in established pattern; on Needle 3, knit.

Repeat Rnds 1 and 2 until the number of stitches equals the number you cast on, then work Rnd 2 only until the sock reaches the base of your big toe. Knit to end of Needle 1; this is now the beginning of the round.

Toe

Rnd 1: K1, ssk, knit to last 3 sts of Needle 2, k2tog, k2, ssk, knit to 3 sts before end of rnd, k2tog, k1—4 stitches decreased.

Rnd 2: Knit.

Repeat Rnds 1 and 2 until you reach the middle of your third toe, then work Rnd 1 until only about 1" (2.5) of sts remain. (Be sure that you have an even number of stitches.) Cut the yarn, leaving a 12" (30.5 cm) tail.

Arrange the remaining stitches on two needles, leaving one extra stitch on the back needle and placing the last stitch worked at the right end of the back needle. Thread the tail on a tapestry needle and use the Kitchener stitch to graft the toe closed:

1. Pass through the first stitch on the front needle as if to knit and slip the stitch off the knitting needle.
2. Pass through the second stitch on the first needle as if to purl, draw the yarn through, and leave the stitch on the needle.
3. Pass through the first stitch on the back needle as if to purl and slip it off.
4. Pass through the second stitch on the back needle as if to knit, draw the yarn through, and leave the stitch on the needle.

Repeat these four steps until all the stitches except one have been slipped off the needles. Pass through the last stitch and fasten off the yarn. Weave in the ends. Block lightly.

Spinning Hemp Bouclé Yarn

In Turkey, bathing is an art form. In the women's bath, women bathe in pairs, each bringing her own *kese* (pronounced KEH-see), a little towel with a loofah-like surface made from linen or tightly spun silk, and a beautiful silver or bronze bowl. Using the kese, the women burnish their skin, pouring steaming water over each other from the little bowls. Between the steam baths, massage, and soaking pools, they have a lovely afternoon indeed.

CHOOSING FIBER

With its antimicrobial qualities and ability to become stronger when wet, hemp seemed the perfect fiber for a New-World kese. A looped novelty yarn is a good choice to make a firm, textured surface perfect for removing all those dead skin cells. Hemp and other bast fibers are easy to spin fine because of the fibers' length.

SPINNING METHOD

I used top and spun a tight, fine single, about 42 wpi and 60 degrees. I spun the fibers worsted; at this length, they simply won't spin easily any other way. I made about 2 ounces (57 grams) on two bobbins.

Using a commercial 20/2 mercerized cotton for the core, I made a push-up looped yarn. 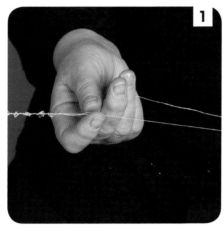 Remember to spin in the direction that the core yarn was plied (in this case, to the left) to make this technique work. When you do so, the

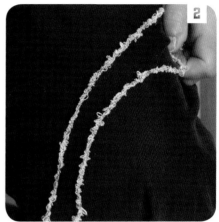

core tightens and the single loosens. The dynamic tension between these two movements forms the loops in the finished yarn. I spun a half bobbin each of singles, about ½ ounce (14 grams) with the core yarn to fill four more bobbins, making sure it had enough twist to be cabled back on itself.

Using these four bobbins, I made a 12-strand cable (4 singles of hemp, 4 strands of 2-ply commercial cotton).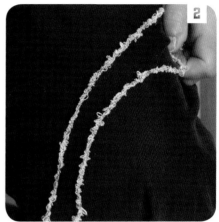

new world kese

Traditional keses are usually narrow bands with a loop at each end for your hands. Of course, you may make your kese any size you like. Traditional keses are woven, but knitting makes a wonderful gently abrasive surface.

FINISHED SIZE
Custom, based on gauge and desired size. Kese shown measures 5" (12.5 cm) wide and 25" (63.5 cm) long.

FIBER
Hemp top; commercial 20/2 cotton.

DRAFTING METHOD
Worsted.

CABLED TWISTS PER INCH
8–10.

CABLED WRAPS PER INCH
5–6.

YARDS PER POUND
300 [274 m].

YARDAGE USED
87 [80 m].

GAUGE
16 sts and 23 rows = 4" [10 cm] in garter stitch.

NEEDLE SIZE
Adjust needle size if necessary to obtain the desired gauge and fabric.

NOTIONS
Tapestry needle.

Knitted Kese

Choose a stitch that will make a firm, tight fabric; I used garter stitch, but firmly knitted moss stitch or basketweave stitch should work nicely. Make a swatch and put it in water to see if it holds its shape well. If it doesn't, use smaller needles.

Using your swatch as a guide, cast on as many stitches as needed for the desired width of your kese (here, 20 stitches). Work until the piece is the desired finished length plus 1" (2.5 cm). Bind off all stitches.

Cable two lengths of 20/2 cotton together to make two cord handles, each about 16" (40.5 cm). Overlap the ends of one handle cord and sew to one end of the kese, then fold over and sew a ½" (1.3 cm) hem to cover handle end. Repeat for other end.

Woven Kese

This is a good project if you're new to weaving. It uses a plain weave and you can work it on a rigid-heddle or other simple loom.

Use a commercial or handspun 20/2 cotton, linen, or hemp warp, set at 10 epi. (If your handspun is on the heavier side, use a 10/2 yarn and a warp set farther apart.) Your sett should let the weft beat in firmly, like a rug, with no warp showing. For each kese you want to weave, you'll need 1½ yards (1.4 m) warp length in addition to your normal loom allowance.

Start by weaving a hem of about 2" (5 cm), using the same thread as the warp. Change to the cabled handspun and weave to the desired length, beating firmly. Weave a 2" (5 cm) hem as for the first end.

Cut off the woven fabric and hand or machine sew across the ends that will be hemmed; repeat with a second seam ¼" (.6 cm) away from the first. (This double row of stitches makes the fabric lie flat.) Wash the fabric in hot water with a little soap. Rinse, dry, and steam press. Make cabled cords as for knitted kese and sew in place on the ends. Turn the hems under, press, and sew in place.

ANN SWANSON

Spin a Wild Fiber Scarf

Qiviut, yak, bison, vicuña, cashmere, wolf, Norwegian Forest cat, chinchilla—the list of true exotic spinning fibers is surprisingly long. Some, like cashmere, qiviut, and bison, are commercially available, but all are in limited supply and are a special spinning treat.

CHOOSING FIBER

For this scarf, I've chosen to spin bison, a fiber that has a deep resonance for me, living as I do on the grasslands of the Great Northern Plains that was once their home. Any fibers with cashmere-like characteristics would work as well. I've used commercially dehaired pure bison down handcarded into rolags. **1 2**

SPINNING HANDSPUN WARP

This scarf is a plain weave, with the heddles threaded straight (1, 2, 3, 4). (It would be simple to make on a rigid-heddle loom.) Because of the fiber and semiwoolen spinning, little of the weaving pattern will show when the scarf is fulled and brushed.

Because I want this scarf to full in the finishing process, I've used a semiwoolen draw. **3** And because I want it to be strong enough for a warp, I've put a very firm twist on the singles. Make sure that you have enough twist by letting the yarn twist back on itself. If the singles aren't spun tightly enough the first time, run them through the wheel again.

As for sock yarn, the highest priority for warp yarn is strength. For your first handspun warp yarns, err on the side of caution, especially if you're a new weaver.

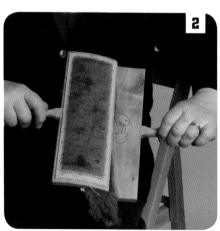

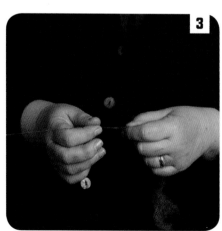

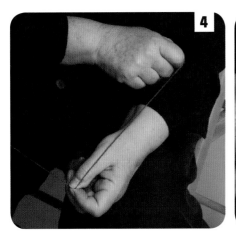
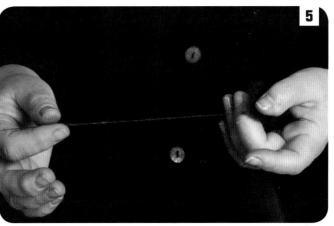

Spin a strong, smooth yarn. **4** Warp yarn should be able to withstand three firm snaps between your hands without breaking. Also like sock yarn, it needs to withstand abrasion. In this case, abrasion would come from the rubbing of the beater against the warp threads as it beats the weft in place and from the heddles as the warp is wound and the cloth is advanced. Warp yarn has to be strong enough not to break as the frames are raised and lowered when the sheds are changed.

I've plied two bobbins of singles firmly. Two-ply is the default yarn when designing a warp because of the way it locks the yarns together in the weaving process. Using a firm ply twist gives the warp a bit more tensile strength and helps it withstand abrasion.

Don't wash the yarn for weaving after plying it—use it straight off the bobbin. In the weaving world, there's a great saying: weaving cloth with a finished yarn is like making an omelet with hard-boiled eggs. If you spritzed your fiber with an oil/water mix while spinning, the oil (along with any oils picked up from your hands during spinning) will act like sizing, and the extra twist that would normally be discharged during the washing will keep it stronger.

After you've used your handspun for warp a few times, experiment. Try softer warps and novelty yarns. The bison yarn that I spun as one element of the scarf warp isn't for the faint of heart. I guarantee a least a few broken threads if you were to wind your warp using only this handspun. However, the resulting fabric would be well worth the annoyance.

SPIN THE WEFT

I used commercially carded bison for my weft yarn, spinning it true woolen with a long draw and plied as for most woolens, **5** with a little more twist in the ply than in the single. As with the warp, I used this yarn as it came off the bobbin.

I spun a sample, wove it on the handspun warp, then fulled it to make sure it was what I needed. I used the sample to estimate how many yards of weft yarn I would need to spin for each scarf. By weighing the bobbin empty and then full, I knew the weight of yarn I needed to spin—in this case, 42 grams per scarf. (For fine fibers, measure weight in grams for accuracy.)

ultra-soft wild fiber scarf

Bison, cashmere, and camels all come from wild, rugged landscapes. Their undercoats keep them warm and toasty when the winds howl and the temperatures plummet. This soft woven scarf will be perfect for winter weather.

I've sett the warp at 24 epi and wound a 10-yard warp, enough for three scarves. Because the warping time and the loom waste are the same for ten scarves as for one, I plan more than one project per warp whenever possible. I've estimated my waste to be 18 inches, or 120 yards of handspun.

To reinforce the warp, I have alternated handspun with a compatible commercial yarn, a 50/50 blend of camel and cashmere down. Because it's stronger than my handspun bison, the commercial yarn works as a supporting structure, taking the warp tension off the bison. The strength of the commercial yarn doesn't come from the fibers, which are shorter and weaker than bison, or from the skill of the spinner (most intermediate spinners can spin the bison as well as a machine). The camel/cashmere yarn is stronger because it has been treated with commercial sizing, which glues the soft surface of the yarn together and protects it from abrasion during weaving. I've used various types of sizing with varying success, but I have yet to find one that works as well on down fibers as the ones used in industrial weaving.

I wove the scarves in plain weave, which makes a lightweight scarf and uses less weft thread than many other patterns do. Use a gentle hand on the beater; think of placing the yarn rather than beating it. If it's difficult to keep the weft from obscuring the warp, consider re-sleying or re-warping; more warp threads per inch makes for lighter cloth and easier beating. I wove these scarves at 20 picks per inch.

FINISHING

Using fulling as the finishing method for short, crimpy fibers that have been spun some variant of woolen helps strengthen the yarns by meshing the fibers together. I removed my scarves from the loom, tied the fringes in small bundles of

FINISHED SIZE
106½ × 6½"
(2.7 m × 16.5 cm).

FIBER
Warp, 100% bison handspun and 50% cashmere/50% camel commercial yarn; weft, 100% bison handspun.

DRAFTING METHOD
Semiwoolen for warp, woolen for weft.

PLIED TWISTS PER INCH
15–18 tpi for warp; 12–16 tpi for weft.

PLIED WRAPS PER INCH
18–20 for warp and weft.

YARDS PER POUND
1,450–1,500 ypp for warp; 1,750–1,800 ypp for weft.

YARDAGE USED
470 yd weft and 1,230 yd each handspun and commercial warp for three scarves.

four strands, and twisted them together in bundles of two. I fulled all three scarves at the same time.

You can full your fabric by machine or by hand. To full in a top-loading washing machine, fill the machine to the appropriate level—entirely covering the fabric but not much higher—with water as hot as possible, add enough good detergent to make the water slippery, and gently agitate the fabric until it starts to mesh together. Let the machine spin the soapy water out, then rinse your fabric pieces in cool water and spin them dry.

If you try fulling by hand, you'll find that a bucket and plunger work just as well as a machine. (I have a sink-sized plunger that I use especially for fulling.) Fill a bucket with hot, soapy water. Use the plunger to agitate the fabric vigorously. **1**

After a few minutes, remove the fabric, rinse it in cold water, then return it to the hot-water bucket and repeat the process. Feel the fabric between your fingers. When it's properly fulled, the warp and weft yarns won't slip easily past one another. Rinse the fabric in cool water and use towels to squeeze most of the water out. **2**

After my scarves had been squeezed and while they were still damp, I gave them a vigorous snap against a hard surface to release the fibers. **3** Although they were still damp, I ironed them firmly, following the line of the warp. I used a bristle brush to nap the fabric, brushing in one direction and then the other, on both sides. (If you find that brushing causes your warp and the weft to move, re-full your fabric.) After brushing, I gave them another hard smack and hung them up to finish drying.

Silk Support

Another simple trick to support a delicate down warp is to carry a fine thread of silk along with the handspun as you wind the warp. Unlike the camel/cashmere blend, which will become part of the pattern of the scarf, the silk thread won't show at all once the fabric is washed and fulled, as in this woven cashmere and qiviut Royal Rat.

Reducing Loom Waste

I could reduce loom waste by about 110 yards (100 meters) by putting on a "dummy" warp. To create one, wind a warp 1 yd (.91 m) long, using any commercial yarn similar in weight to your actual warp. Sley the commercial warp through the reed, thread the heddles, and tie it on the back beam. Tie your actual warp onto the dummy and pull it gently through the reed and heddles, then wind on your warp as you normally would. For this warp, a dummy would save about 50 yards of handspun; if I had chosen to make the whole warp handspun, I would have saved 100 yards.

caring for your work

Getting (and Keeping) the Pests Out

Insects are the most prolific inhabitants of the earth and our constant companions. Conditions that suit humans—coastal, temperate, humid—are perfect for most insects. They are the ultimate recyclers; what is to us a gorgeous handspun, handknitted wool sweater or a beautiful pair of fur-lined gloves is from an insect's perspective dead and discarded hair and skin to be eaten and recycled. When it happens outdoors, it's useful and necessary; when it happens indoors to our fiber stash and textile collections, it's a disaster.

The two insect pests that most concern textile collectors and fiber artists are clothes moths and carpet beetles. The methods that protect fibers from damage are the same for both insects. These pests attack the same materials, the keratins and chitins that make up most of our protein fiber. Silk is not attractive to or digestible by insects; however, both moths and carpet beetles will eat through silk that is covering keratin fibers or has been dyed with insects such as cochineal and lac.

CARPET BEETLES

Carpet beetles are nearly indestructible. Although not often found in raw fleece, they can cause great destruction to a textile collection (and especially to carpets, of course). Carpet beetles are often brought into the house and studio on cut flowers or the fur of pets.

The three major species of carpet beetles are the varied carpet beetle, the common carpet beetle, and the black carpet beetle. Despite many additional regional varieties, all carpet beetles are fairly similar. They're most often small, beautifully marked beetles with a wide range of intricately patterned yellow, red, and black stripes, but they can also be black or brown. All of them are a menace and should be dealt with as soon as possible.

Although the full-grown beetle is the most visible stage of this insect's life cycle, adult beetles feed only on pollen and nectar. The larva does the textile damage. Carpet beetle larvae and eggs can survive a wide range of conditions. They can survive freezing temperatures for at least three

Peruvian dolls made from pre-contact grave cloth.

years, returning quickly from dormancy with a rise in temperature. They survive heat and are active at 105° Fahrenheit (41° Celsius). And they can withstand long periods of starvation.

CLOTHES MOTHS

Only two species of moths are a threat to fibers: the casemaking clothes moth and the common clothes moth. If you spot a moth in the house, capture it and make sure that you have a problem before you worry. The casemaking moth can be identified by the brown spots on the forewing. Clothes moths, however, are easily confused with outdoor moths and pantry or meal moths.

If the source of the flying moth is stored grains, flour, or pet food, it is almost certainly a meal moth. The meal moth has a dark, pointed head and a distinctly two-toned wing. Clothes moths are light colored, with a silvery white to pale rosy-brown color, and they fly in a fluttering, drunken manner. They measure about ¼ inch (6 millimeters) in length. At rest, they hold their

carpet beetle

ANDRÉ KARWATH

long, narrow wings close to their bodies; the ends of the wings are often scalloped.

Although the adult moths don't feed, the larvae can do an extraordinary amount of damage in a short period of time. The larvae are a glossy creamy white with brown heads that measure about ⅓ inch (1 centimeter) when full grown. They have feet, although the feet aren't noticeable. The casemaking moth spins a tight cylinder that can cover its body, which it pulls along as it travels to feed. The common clothes moth larva spins a tentlike covering (sometimes referred to as a tunnel or burrow) that it lives beneath. I've seen moth casings made with paper, fiberglass, plastic bags, acrylic yarn, and silk, all fibers the moths were unable to digest but chewed up all the same.

INSECT PREVENTION

The best defense against insect damage is diligence and an immediate response. If you see a casemaking or common clothes moth flying, it means there's an infestation. These moths don't fly unless they're disturbed or need to find a less crowded place to lay their eggs. Check immediately for the source, which

common clothes moth

OLAF LEILLINGER

should be close by because the moths don't fly very far. Be ruthless in removing the source! Most fiber can be replaced (or suitably mourned).

It's easy to kill an insect in its flying, pupa, or larval stage. Freezing, heat, and most pesticides will work just fine. The eggs, however, are made to survive. Insect eggs are hard to find; what you can see, the small round pellets, are *fraize* (scat). Research isn't clear about whether washing will remove the eggs entirely, but it's clear that anything that will kill an insect egg will be dangerous to you. The best way to avoid an insect infestation is prevention. The strategies I describe

won't actually kill an insect egg, but they will discourage them from moving in.

Make Your Textiles Uninviting

Carpet beetles and moths don't like light, they don't like to be disturbed, and they don't like it dry. Avoid using baskets to store your beautiful skeins and fibers; if you do, line them with plastic or smooth cotton cloth. Every three to six months, vacuum and wash your baskets with soapy water. Move your work around. Vacuum the front and back of tapestries, wall hangings, and rugs. Hang all pieces away from walls so that light can get behind them.

Peruvian bag, nature-dyed alpaca, nineteenth century. The rare patterns indicate it was woven near Cuzco. The twentieth-century strap repair was done with synthetically dyed yarn.

Use packs of desiccants, available at craft stores, to absorb moisture in storage boxes. Doing so won't kill insect eggs but it will help keep them from hatching.

Dry cleaning is a surprisingly successful way to destroy moth populations in wool textiles, not because the chemicals are toxic to the eggs (as they once were) but because the larvae can't survive on clean wool. Although keratin is their only source of protein and the main part of their diet, they also need the sugars found either on raw wool or in sweat, food, or urine stains, all of which are completely removed by dry cleaning. Not all textiles are suitable for dry cleaning, however; some may be too frail to withstand the tumbling process, and nature-dyed colors can be changed by dry-cleaning materials.

Make Textiles Unrecognizable

Moths find keratin and chitin by smell; if you can block the smell of the protein, the moths will avoid your textiles and fibers unless they're desperate. Adult moths don't eat, but for the survival of their offspring, they seek out a good food supply, so that when the eggs hatch there's plenty of food on hand. Moth repellents work by discouraging moths from laying their eggs because they can't recognize the protein smell. Lavender, wormwood, and cedar are good examples of odors that block the smell of keratin and chitin. Store primitive fleece, natural-colored fleece, raw (unwashed) fleeces, and naturally dyed fleece and objects separate from your main stash. Practice extra diligence with these because all have a strong odor that attracts moths.

Make Your Stash Impenetrable

Plastic is available in all forms. Heavy plastic containers, such as five-gallon pails, ice cream buckets, and heavyweight bags, will defeat any moth. If you're anxious that off-gassing will affect your fibers, textiles, or even you, choose containers that are classed as food safe. If you're concerned about environmental responsibility, look for recycled plastic or reuse containers that would be thrown away.

Create a Quarantine Area

As an extra precaution, isolate any incoming fleeces, yarns, and other textiles for several weeks if possible. Store them in separate trash barrels or heavy-duty plastic bags. Keep them warm to see if any insects appear; moths hatch above 70° Fahrenheit (21° Celcius). As an added precaution, I fumigate any antique pieces in my "killing trunk," a metal storage trunk with a dichlorvos strip (see page 141) attached to the lid. I'm very cautious about using chemicals, but for old pieces that are irreplaceable, I think it's necessary. I keep this trunk sealed with tape to contain the chemical and air the piece well before hanging it.

INSECT ELIMINATION MYTHS

Anything that's powerful enough to harm an insect can harm you. The following common suggestions for eliminating insects are, alas, apocryphal and ineffective.

1 *Storing your fleece layered between newspapers will kill insects.* It did indeed when printing ink was still made with lead, which killed the eggs before they hatched. But the lead wasn't good for us either, and it has been banned from use in ink in most developed nations.

2 *Freezing kills moths.* Sadly not. Moth eggs are designed to survive and will withstand temperatures well below 0° Fahrenheit (minus 18° Celsius) for several years. Even larvae can stand temperatures of 40° Fahrenheit (4° Celsius); they simply become comatose, then resume eating within a few seconds when the temperature rises.

3 *Hot sunshine kills moths.* Moths can withstand a great deal of heat, up to 120° Fahrenheit (49° Celsius). Although larvae don't like bright light and will move quite rapidly to escape sunlight, it doesn't affect the eggs at all.

4 *Lavender, aromatic cedar, and other herbal remedies kill moths.* Again, sadly not, although they are effective deterrents.

5 *Store your wool so air can move through it and the wool can breathe.* In my experience, wool lasts much longer tightly packed. If it's able to "breathe," it might breathe in moths or mice.

EFFECTIVE MOTH AND BEETLE ELIMINATORS

It's easier to prevent an infestation than to cure it. Getting rid of pests once they appear requires serious chemical intervention.

Moth Crystals, Balls, or Flakes

Moth crystals are made with either naphthalene or paradichlorobenzene, both of which have been used effectively for a long time. They both emit a gas that's heavier than air, so use them above whatever material you want to protect. Used fresh and in an enclosed space, they kill all flying moths, larvae, and eggs. Spread around in an open space, they act as a repellent. They should be used with caution, however, and material treated with moth crystals should be well aired before it's used.

Dichlorvos-Impregnated Strips

Developed originally for use around livestock and in food preparation areas, these strips are odorless, long lasting, and incredibly effective. They're also toxic and should be handled with extreme care. Hung in a storage area, they kill all flying insects; in an enclosed space, they also kill all larvae and eggs.

Professional Fumigation

If you have a serious infestation, call a professional. Your local museum may be able to suggest someone or a firm that's knowledgeable and reliable. Make a note of the chemicals used. It often takes several treatments to rid you of these bothersome pests.

Mice

If you live in an agricultural area, you soon realize that mice are an extremely important part of our ecological system, and the land would be barren indeed without mice. Wool is their preferred nesting material.

You'll know right away if your storage area has a mouse infestation; the smell is unmistakable. Like moths, mice reproduce rapidly, and diligence and quick response on your part are your best defenses. If you do have a mouse infestation, be careful cleaning it up. Ruthlessly remove all the soiled material. Use soap and water to wash down the area and make sure mice cannot get back into your storage.

In many parts of the American West, deer mice sometimes carry the hantavirus, and exposure to wet or dried mouse urine is dangerous. Check with your local public health unit to see if you need to take extra precautions when cleaning up. The most ecologically sound method of mouse prevention (and my preferred method) is a good mousing cat, but if you can't stem the mouse damage (especially in an area of hantavirus), you can choose from the wide variety of mouse poisons and traps on the market to keep your storage area mouse free.

Wool Storage

My methods of wool storage are based on my experiences in the wool industry working as a wool classer and handler for a shearing company. Using a square packer, a piece of equipment that reduces 500 pounds (227 kilograms) of wool into a woven-nylon-covered bale that measures about 4 feet (1.2 meters) square, I baled hundreds of thousands of pounds of wool. The bales had to be rock-hard; when I kicked them with my boot, they needed to sound like wood and feel like cement.

This system makes the bales easy to transport, but I was interested to learn that wool lasts for years in a well-packed bale. Baled raw wool from my area of Montana is often shipped to South Carolina, where it may sit outside for several years. Rain, moths, and mice might penetrate the outer surface to $1/16$ inch (2 millimeter) depth, but when opened, the rest of the bale is as fresh as the day it was shorn.

Seeing how the bales worked revolutionized my own fleece-storage system. Even if your storage is mouse and moth free, oxygen can change unwashed fleece. When oxygen interacts with wool waxes and oils, they start to decompose and crystallize. These changes make the fleece much more difficult to scour, and the wool is often described as "sticky" or "tacky." If the oils and waxes have been washed out of your fleece, it can be exposed to oxygen without harm, but it will still be affected by light. All light—natural light, fluorescent light, and ultraviolet light—can cause fiber deterioration.

Simply storing fleeces in closed plastic bags in direct sunlight can cause serious moisture damage. A fresh fleece, no matter what the animal source, contains a fairly high amount of water, especially in a damp climate. As a loosely packed fleece heats up, the fleece sweats off some of the water, which can accumulate in the bag and cause the wool to mold. If the wool is tightly packed, the amount of sweating decreases significantly.

I've chosen to store wool tightly packed. I use recycled airtight plastic pails to store special fleeces. You would be surprised at how much wool can be tightly packed into a pail; a five-gallon bucket will hold about 6 pounds (2.7 kilograms). The buckets stack well and are impervious to moths and mice. I write the date on the pail and tape on a sample lock of the fleece.

Protection for Textiles

Protecting your own work and your textile collection is similar in many ways to protecting your fiber.

Textiles need to be protected from all forms of unnecessary light, insect pests, mice, water damage, and environmental contaminants such as smoke and other chemical fumes. For most textiles, plastic boxes that seal well are perfectly fine.

For special textiles that you have stewardship of, check into museum-quality storage boxes, which are ideal (if a little expensive). In either type of box, use plenty of layers of acid-free paper to protect and cushion textile pieces. Whenever possible, roll your textiles instead of folding them because during long storage the folds and creases can become permanent weak spots. Cover a heavy cardboard tube or sturdy plastic pipe with acid-free paper and roll your pieces. Roll them with the good side out; it will have less stress on the fabric. Wrap the rolls in acid-free paper and place them in your storage containers.

STORAGE AREAS

Ideally, store your pieces in a separate closed-off area. If you feel comfortable with chemicals, a dichlorvos-impregnated strip will give you extra protection. If possible, store new additions to your

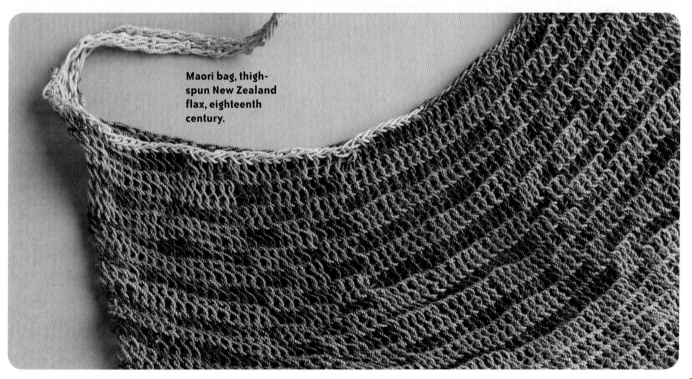

Maori bag, thigh-spun New Zealand flax, eighteenth century.

collection separately until you're sure they haven't brought any pests with them (1½ to 2 months), especially keratin-based materials.

Check your storage area often and keep it clean—vacuum, vacuum, vacuum. Make sure that when you store pieces they're clean; remember that moths love sweat and food stains. They also are attracted to insect-based dyes. A lovely tapestry from Peru that had a magical pattern of cochineal-dyed ladybugs was once brought to me for restoration. Sadly, most of the ladybugs were gone, and those that remained were covered with larvae. The larvae had eaten exactly to the pattern of the cochineal dye.

Remember: Don't count on cedar-lined closets and chests to kill moths. They help keep moths away, but won't kill them.

DISPLAY

Whether you're displaying textiles that you've collected or pieces that you created yourself, fabrics need a little extra care to keep them from being damaged. For very special pieces, you may want to go to a professional framer with textile experience, but with a little patience most textile pieces can be mounted in your studio.

For pieces to be hung without framing, make sure that they're hung far enough from the wall so the textile doesn't touch the wall. This approach protects pieces from any chemical in the wall finish and allows a little light and air movement behind the piece, which helps discourage moth and beetle infestations.

A simple way to hang a piece such as a rug or tapestry is to cover a 2 × 4 cut to the right length with linen, then sew a strip of Velcro across it. Stitch the opposite Velcro strip onto the back of the piece you want to mount, using a blunt- or round-tipped needle and sturdy thread. Be careful when you're sewing not to pierce the warp threads of any woven piece; careful handsewing does little damage and is reversible. Mount the 2 × 4 board to the wall; mount the textile to the Velcro on the board. It's easy to remove the piece for cleaning if you pull it sideways but impossible to move if you tug down on it. To prevent longer pieces from leaning in toward the wall at the bottom, place synthetic household sponges at intervals behind the piece; they'll grip both the piece and the wall without being visible.

If you decide to frame a textile piece, mount it on a piece of high-density fiberboard covered with linen or silk material. Avoid using cardboard, which can contain acids harmful to the fabric. Pin the textile to the linen or silk backing, making sure that the pins go between and not through the threads of the textile being preserved. Also be sure that the textile piece is mounted straight, following the lines of the warp (if it's woven) or the stitches (if it's knitted). When you have it properly pinned in place, use button-weight cotton or linen thread and an overhand stitch to secure it in place all the way around. This process is a bit painstaking, but it is well worth the effort. When you choose a frame, look for one with a deep rebate so that the framed textile will never touch the glass. (This is the same framing method used for pastel artwork.) For some pieces for which it would be interesting to see both sides, a window can be cut into the matting material. Covered with Plexiglas, this allows the back to be viewed as well. In all cases, be careful to use a damp cloth to clean the glass to avoid static, which can draw the fibers in a thread toward the yarn strongly enough to damage the piece.

LIGHT

Textiles are mounted and hung to be seen and enjoyed, but you must protect them from unnecessary and harmful exposure to light. Light can fade both natural-colored and dyed material by causing the structure of the fiber to change. The safe level of light for textiles is 50 lux (the international unit of illumination); sunlight streaming in on a summer day is about 100,000 lux. Try to keep your textiles away from direct sunlight. Artificial light is also harmful, especially fluorescent lights without special filters. Ordinary electric bulbs are the least harmful. Consider rotating your pieces in and out of your safe (and pest-free) storage area—it's refreshing to see new work and rotation protects your pieces from light exposure.

Records

Being a good steward of the textiles you have collected requires more than just keeping them safe from damage. If you have a collection of textile treasures, be sure to record the information you have about them using your camera and computer (or a pen and a file card). Record what they are, where they came from, how they were made, and any other details you might have. Objects often survive us, but too commonly the information we have about them is lost.

Be as good a steward of your own work. Make it a practice to keep detailed records of your work. Make notes about the materials and techniques you used, how long the project took, what you were happy with, and what you would change. Take pictures of skeins and finished pieces. These records will be valuable to you when you want to do a similar project, but more importantly, they help build knowledge about textiles and the role they play in modern life.

As a teacher, I've heard so many wonderful stories about people's work—not just the how of it, which is interesting in itself, but also the why of it. Why, in the age of industrialization, do we still want to make cloth by hand? One woman, a wonderful spinner and knitter, raveled the two cashmere sweaters she had inherited from her mother, cabled the fine yarns together, dyed them magical colors, and lovingly knitted a three-generation sweater for her granddaughter. Another woman spun and wove a fine wool blanket in strips like kente cloth for her African-American daughter to take with her to college. A beautiful shawl for a bride, a Buddhist mandala on a silk pile bag, a pair of socks made while traveling in Europe— these pieces all have stories to tell, stories that form another fabric, equally valuable, equally worth preserving. Just write them down.

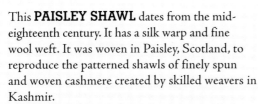

This **PAISLEY SHAWL** dates from the mid-eighteenth century. It has a silk warp and fine wool weft. It was woven in Paisley, Scotland, to reproduce the patterned shawls of finely spun and woven cashmere created by skilled weavers in Kashmir.

In the middle years of the eighteenth century, the East India Company brought intricately woven shawls from Kashmir to Britain and thus brought cashmere fiber to the attention of the European fashion industry. The shawls became a required piece of clothing for every "woman of quality" for the next century. An authentic shawl was a significant investment. The price (in the 1700s, they cost a minimum of 500 pounds) and rarity made for great competition among European mills to see who could be the first to adapt their machinery to produce them. The ornate patterns were not a problem to reproduce; British mills at that time had the ability to weave the complex patterns. What made the Kashmir shawls so different and so desirable was the fiber. Try as they might, they could not find spinning or weaving machinery that could handle the fine, soft fiber, nor could they find a comparable sheep's wool. Eventually, a mill in Paisley, Scotland, was one of the first to be able to weave a material similar to the original shawls. Paisley and Scotland still play a major role in the cashmere world.

The effort to produce less expensive Kashmir-style shawls also had an impact on sheep. When the equipment changed to spin and weave delicate fibers, so did the sheep. From that time on, Merino sheep were bred for finer and finer fleeces until they became the Merinos we know today, with a similar (but still not quite the same) hand as cashmere.

There was another surprising result of the attempt to replicate Kashmir shawls. Now ubiquitous, finely spun cotton sewing thread has not been available for very long. The first cotton thread produced for sale was made by the Clark brothers of Paisley. In the early 1800s, the silk that had been used for heddles became unavailable during the Napoleonic Wars. In 1806, Patrick Clark developed a way to spin very smooth, strong thread from cotton. It was only by chance that he discovered that the thread could also be used for sewing, and they began selling it commercially in 1812. A few years later, James Coats, who also worked in Paisley, set up his own factory to make high-quality sewing thread. Over a century later, the two companies merged into one of the world's largest and best-known needlecraft companies.

Holding my beautiful shawl, I have history in my hands. Tracing its path from the Himalayas to the courts of Europe to the sheep stations of the Australian outback to my studio here in the Pacific Northwest, I see how the development of the simple, perfect thread that makes this intricate fabric has both transformed the world around us and formed a web that links it—and us—together.

bibliography and further reading

Barber, E.J.W. *Prehistoric Textiles: The Development of Cloth in the Neolithic and Bronze Ages with Special Reference to the Aegean.* Princeton, New Jersey: Princeton University Press, 1991.

Botkin, M.P., Ray A. Field, and C. Leroy Johnson. *Sheep and Wool: Science, Production, and Management.* Englewood Cliffs, New Jersey: Prentice Hall, 1988.

Budiansky, Stephen. *The Covenant of the Wild: Why Animals Chose Domestication.* New York: William Morrow, 1992.

———. *The Nature of Horses: Exploring Equine Evolution, Intelligence, and Behavior.* New York: Free Press, 1997.

Fannin, Allen. *Handspinning Art & Technique.* New York: Van Nostrand Reinhold, 1970.

Finch, Karen, and Greta Putnam. *Caring for Textiles.* London: Barrie & Jenkins, 1977.

Forbes, R.J. *Studies in Ancient Technology. Vol. 4, The Fibres and Fabrics of Antiquity.* Leiden, Netherlands: Brill, 1955.

Kinsman, David James John. *Black Sheep of Windermere: A History of the St. Kilda or Hebridean Sheep.* Windermere: Windy Hall Publications, 2001.

Ryder, M.L. *Sheep & Man.* London: Duckworth, 1983.

Ryder, M.L. ,and S.K. Stephenson. *Wool Growth.* New York: Academic Press, 1968.

Simpson, W.S., and G.H. Crawshaw, eds. *Wool: Science and Technology.* Cambridge, England: Woodhead, 2002.

Stewart, Hilary. *Cedar: Tree of Life to the Northwest Coast Indians.* Seattle: University of Washington Press, 1984.

———. *Indian Fishing: Early Methods on the Northwest Coast.* Seattle: University of Washington Press, 1977.

Ulrich, Laurel Thatcher. *A Midwife's Tale: The Life of Martha Ballard, Based on Her Diary, 1785–1812.* New York: Knopf, 1990.

Weiner, Annette B., and Jane Schneider, eds. *Cloth and Human Experience.* Washington, D.C.: Smithsonian Institution Press, 1989.

Wingate, Isabel B. *Textile Fabrics and Their Selection.* New York: Prentice Hall, 1942.

credits

The publisher gratefully acknowledges the following people and companies for their contributions to the book:

Front cover, pages 60, 64: Schacht-Reeves spinning wheel provided by Schacht Spindle Co. Inc.

Contents, page 10: Photograph courtesy of the Flax Council of Canada and Flax Canada 2015

page 10: Cotton provided by Phreadde Davis

page 13, top left: Photograph by Geof Kime of Stemergy.com

page 14: Antique flax hackle provided by Debi Dodge

page 19: Photographs of cotton by Phreadde Davis

page 20: Photograph of cotton courtesy of *Spin·Off* Magazine

page 32: Photograph of pygora goat by Lisa Roskopf of Hawks Mountain Ranch

page 36: Photograph of paco-vicuña by Phil Switzer of Switzer-Land Alpacas

page 39: Photograph of bison courtesy of Buffalo Gold, buffalogold.net

page 40, back cover: Photograph of yak by Patti Juuti, Canadian Yak Products, Rimbey, Alberta, spjuuti@mac.com

page 43: Photograph of reeling silk courtesy of Michael Cook, wormspit.com

page 44: Photograph of bombyx moth by Michael Cook, wormspit.com

page 47: Bamboo scarf by Laura Fry

pages 49–56: Yarn by Patsy Sue Zawistoski, spinninguru.com

page 52: Corn and corn fiber provided by Liz Gipson

page 72 (top): Fiber provided by Liz Gipson

pages 82, 105: Yarn by Jeane deCoster

page 84: Bobbin winder provided by Schacht Spindle Co. Inc.

page 104, bottom left: Fiber provided by Beth Smith, The Spinning Loft, thespinningloft.com

page 104, crimp meter: The Duerden scale is reproduced with the permission of Australian Wool Innovation Limited, owner of The Woolmark Company, member of IWS Nominee.

pages 106–107: Spinning flowchart and pulley selection diagram based on original charts by Shane and Shiori Hatagawa.

page 109: Knitted sweater by Kathryn Alexander

page 135: Royal Rat by Karin Jackson

page 138: Common clothes moth photograph by Olaf Leillinger (used under Creative Commons license and GNU Free Documentation License; see creativecommons.org/licenses/by-sa/2.5/ and commons.wikimedia.org/wiki/Commons:GNU_Free_Documentation_License)

page 138: Carpet beetle photograph by André Karwath (used under Creative Commons license; see creativecommons.org/licenses/by-sa/2.5/

Back cover: Knitted silk cap by Jean Cleavinger

Thanks to Shuttles, Spindles, and Skeins of Boulder, Colorado, for providing equipment and supplies for photography.

index

inspiring resources from interweave

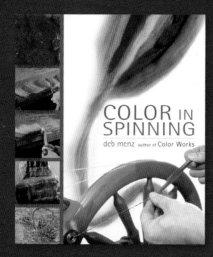

**Start Spinning:
Everything You Need to
Know to Make Great Yarn**
Maggie Casey, $21.95
ISBN 978-1-59668-065-4

**Color in
Spinning**
Deb Menz, $26.95
ISBN 978-1-931499-82-8

**The Spinner's
Companion**
Bobbie Irwin, $19.95
ISBN: 978-1-883010-79-9

also from interweave

Spin·off
it's about making yarn by hand

the magazine that highlights the vibrant
and diverse spinning community and
explores the intricacies of the craft.

spinoffmagazine.com